WING CHUN
LIFE PHYSICS

JONATHAN **PRITCHARD**

Front cover image by Jonathan Pritchard
Book design by Jonathan Pritchard

Printed by Like A Mind Reader, in the United States of America.

ISBN: 978-0-9823708-6-5

www.WingChun.life
thrive@wingchun.life

To the many who have come before.

OTHER BOOKS BY
JONATHAN **PRITCHARD**

[think] Like A Mind Reader

[Learn] Like A Mind Reader

Perfect **Recall**

(all available on Amazon.com)

CONTENTS

INTRODUCTION

"When we try to pick out anything by itself, we find it hitched to everything else in the Universe."

~John Muir

When I first read this quote years ago I took it as a trite comment on the interconnectedness of all things. When I saw it again after starting this book, I saw it for the flash of brilliance it truly is. Every time I thought of a subject I wanted to cover in this book, it would connect with five more topics, which in turn sprouted their own branches.

What started as a relatively straightforward concept for a book immediately expanded at a geometric rate to include topics that, at first glance, would seem like a total non sequitur for a book on how to punch and kick.

It got to the point where I kept a marker in the shower so I could record ideas as they flooded my mind, non-stop. Fortunately I never got to the point of writing on the walls, but I was seriously tempted more than once.

This is a big book for any topic, let alone Kung Fu. But in order to communicate the sheer genius of the Wing Chun system and its capacity to revolutionize the world, I felt it was only right to at least give you a hint at how applicable the principles & strategies embedded in the system truly are across domains.

And it really is just a hint.

Every day it seems like I find some new insight that's been waiting patiently for me to see as it sat in plain sight since day one. These are just the whispers of intuition that I've heard during my daily practice. What speaks to you now, quietly, from these pages will eventually wind up shouting at you from every part of your life if you put these ideas into action.

I know it will happen to you, because that is exactly what happened to me.

We'll start by explaining what Wing Chun is on a surface level, and then we'll broaden out to see how the same concepts ripple out into relationships, business, health, cognitive fallacies, and more. Its reach is far and wide, but starting narrow will give us the best chance of making sense of the broad picture.

There's only so much you can know from reading, however. Living these principles will reveal more to you than 100 lifetimes of just thinking about this stuff. But starting with the right approach will get you more out of this life than 1,000 lifetimes of practicing with the wrong mindset.

What began as a 'how-to' book on Kung Fu transitioned into a book on masculinity, philosophy, friendship, physics, mathematics, and all manner of interconnected vertices.

Which is a long way of saying this is a book about Kung Fu.

Hands up, head down, eyes sharp.

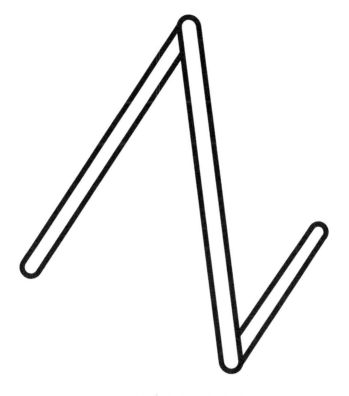

THEORY

the·o·ry

THirē/noun

1: a supposition or a system of ideas intended to explain something, especially one based on general principles independent of the thing to be explained.

What Do You Want?

This is an essential question you have to answer before you dive in. What do you want out of reading this book? Are you casually interested in this punching and kicking stuff? Do you want to learn some new exercises to get fit? Do you want to work on your cardio? Are you looking to face a bully at school? At work? Are you training to step into the octagon?

What's your motivation for learning more about this system? If you don't have an answer to that question, I can't give you any answers.

Maybe there are several reasons. Maybe you have one reason now, and another one later.

Every time you read this book it will change because you will change more and more as you apply its principles in your own life. Feel free to use this as a reference book that you continue to come back to in moments of difficulty.

Or, even better, come back when things are

good to rediscover the wisdom hidden between the words that you'll only unlock as you apply the ideas and learn from the experiences.

One line that never stood out to you the first couple times reading through will suddenly glow like it's radioactive. You'll wonder how in the world you could have missed something so obvious.

That's the wisdom of experience being revealed to you. That means you're learning.

That means you're living Kung Fu.

Punch *Me*

"What?"

"Don't worry about it. Just punch me. Go for it."

"Alright, if you say so."

He readied himself, and launched a fist as hard as he could at his best friend.

They were in the same grade, exactly the same

height, exactly the same weight, and exactly the same build.

But his best friend practiced Karate after school three times a week.

He didn't.

What started as absolute confidence revealed itself as arrogance and quickly transformed to absolute confusion as the horizon, sky, and ground all conspired to violate the laws of physics. They tumbled and turned in an impossible dance.

He was flying through the air but his poor brain couldn't make sense of it.

He landed on his back.

Hard.

The air was knocked completely out of his lungs, but it was a small price to pay if it meant his world would stop spinning.

"Breathe out" his friend said, bending over him. Smiling. "You can't breathe in, so breathe out. It'll get your breath back."

Soon his wits returned, and he rediscovered "up." He jumped to his feet.

"Do it again!" he shouted, even more eager this time.

His best friend smiled, only too happy to oblige his willing victim.

Chapter 1

On Quality

If I asked you about Quality[1] you'd know right away what idea I'm talking about, but if I asked you to explain what it is, you might find the harder you try to pin it down the more fuzzy it gets. Basically, we could bet on most people saying it's one thing being better than something else.

But how do you know?

Is there some sort of universal standard definition of "good" and "not good" that we're all born with? Or is it something that depends on the context before you can know if something is good Quality, or not?

One of the books I read in my younger years that heavily influenced my thinking of what, exactly, Quality is all about is Robert Pirsig's *"Zen and the Art of Motorcycle Maintenance."*

---

[1]   Just like the word 'Tao' is consistently capitalized for being a universal principle or idea, I consistently capitalize 'Quality' for much the same reason. This is to differentiate the universal Quality from the momentary understand of a good or bad quality thing or idea.

It's an incredible book, and there's a reason it spawned so many "Zen and the art of" clones over the years. A quick search on Amazon showed me results ranging from Zen and the Art of "Archery," "Making a Deal," "Happiness," "Making a Living," "Fundraising," and best of all I found this gem: Zen and the Art of "Faking It."

But there's a reason *Zen and the Art of Motorcycle Maintenance* is still at the top of the pile. Pirsig digs into the nature of Quality by telling a story of travel, fatherhood, insanity, and losing himself through electroshock therapy.

The book is largely autobiographical.

Objective vs Subjective Reality

When you look into the nature of reality for any length of time, like Pirsig, you start from a place that totally makes sense, but you wind up somewhere you never expected. A truly puzzling idea you land on is the inherent subject/object dichotomy of the universe. There's an objective 'out there' and individual 'subjects' who experience it.

It makes perfect sense that there's an objective reality regardless of anyone being around to enjoy it (subjective experience). Objective reality really exists. You can measure it. It's the world of particles, atoms, molecules, stars, and celestial bodies.

Subjective experience doesn't exist in the same way. You can't measure it. There's no thermometer for happy, or sad, or betrayal, or justice, but they feel real. They're metaphysical. They exist in a realm beyond the observable nature of reality.

This is why the Zen koan of "if a tree falls in the forest, does it still make a sound?" makes no sense. Of course objective reality continues without an observer! But ask yourself this: where does objective reality meet the observer? Or, another way of putting it: Where does experience meet the mind?

This is the quagmire of thinking about Quality. You can't define it. It's inherently a perceptual experience that happens before you can form any idea about what it is you're experiencing. Quality is, itself, the direct engagement with experience and reality. It's what all the mind hacking gurus call 'flow.'

It's all just another word for Quality.

It's the fundamental force that gives rise to everything in the universe; both physical and metaphysical.

If you don't understand how Quality is, itself, the singular force that creates the universe[2], you'll be understandably confused if you think Quality is just 'whatever you like.' The subjective-only understanding of Quality means there's no universal standard for evaluating what is good or bad.

If, however, you say there's an objective standard of Quality, then where is it? Point to it. Show me. If it's objectively real, you should be able to measure it just like you can measure temperature, mass, weight, and every other *real* thing in the

---

2   Objective reality and Subjective reality. Physical and Metaphysical.

universe.

But, neither of those approaches feels right, do they?

Imagine you're given two stories. One is written by a professional, and the other is the work of an amateur who just started writing six months ago. Even if you have zero experience in writing stories yourself, you'll instantly be able to tell the difference between them.

The Quality between the two will be blatantly obvious.

So, what's going on?

Pirsig's insight was Quality precedes the separation of Subject/Object. There's no difference between the experience and the experiencer. It's two parts of the whole thing called 'reality.'

His argument is Quality is a direct experience of reality, **before** the experiencer can separate the experience from the person experiencing it.

Think about it long enough, like he did, and you'll realize there are really two types of Quality: Dynamic and Static. Dynamic Quality is the direct in-the-moment flow of being here and now. It's like being totally engaged with a symphony, or being moved by an incredible painting.

Static Quality, however, is the result of a dynamic experience becoming codified, or trapped, in an idea, belief, memory, etc. It's being able to think about how moved you were, or appreciating how the painter used classic principles of composition in a surprising way. It's everything that we can know, understand, and write down. Dynamic Quality is experienced. Static Quality is understood.

The 10 Commandments are a Static Quality pattern, whereas living by them is Dynamic Quality. Words in a dictionary are Static Quality. The actual physical objects, animals, experiences, and ideas those words represent are Dynamic Quality. If you can define it, it's Static Quality. If you're experiencing it, it's Dynamic Quality.

Static Quality is our codified ideas, systems, beliefs, and ideals. They're born, first, in patterns at the inorganic level, then biological, then social, and finally at the intellectual level.

Evolution is the inexorable process of Static Quality patterns realizing higher-level Quality patterns, and we call this progress morality. This is why we think a deer eating salt is perfectly moral. It's a biological pattern overcoming an inorganic pattern. And it's why a higher Static Quality pattern called 'person' can take antibiotics, an inorganic Static Quality pattern, to kill a lower Static Quality pattern 'bacteria' that is causing problems. Quality is the reason it's OK for an idea to overcome a social norm. Intellectual patterns are a higher Static Quality pattern than social customs.

OK. We're pretty far out there for a book on Wing Chun, I know, but it all pays off, I promise. You're with me so far, and you might be wondering, "So, what makes all this Quality stuff happen? What causes something to be high value, or low value?"

That is a deceptively complex question you're asking.

Now we're getting into the realm of causality. "What causes good or bad?" It's a simple question that has plagued thinkers from the beginning of time. Aristotelian philosophy says that 'cause' means "an explanation for," or "the answer to a why question."

What causes things to happen? Why does A cause B?

Pirsig had another insight: there is no causality. It's all patterns of value that are the result of Quality.

Instead of thinking 'A causes B,' Pirsig asserts 'B values preconditions A.' It's a small linguistic change, and feels really clunky when you first read it, but all manner of causality-related issues evaporate once you understand a Quality value-pattern-first framework of explaining reality.

Gravity doesn't cause water to flow downhill. The pattern of value we call "water" values "downhill" more than "uphill," as gravity or "downness" is a universal moral Quality pattern.

Seeing the world through a Quality 'pattern of value' lens is like seeing the fundamental code of the Matrix for the first time.

With a values-based world view, you'll realize that everything is a pattern of value. Every single atom, molecule, creature, society, law, and idea is simply a pattern and expression of values. Then you'll realize that the patterns of value that align most closely with universal patterns of value are the highest-Quality patterns, and therefore the most moral.

The more universally applicable the value pattern, the higher Quality it is. Universal principles[3] never contradict themselves and never violate other universal principles; they're

---

3   Universal patterns of Static Quality.

interconnected and congruent.

The laws of gravity are the same on Earth as they are on Jupiter as they are on any of the thousands of exoplanets we've discovered. Physics governs the dance between stars and their planets along with the planets and their moons with perfect equality.

The laws discovered by Newton are the same here as they are anywhere in the known universe.

There are no exceptions.

Their universality is what makes them the highest-Quality pattern of value possible. Other patterns that value these universal constants make them high Quality, too.

And all this stuff is precisely what Kung Fu is all about. It's the highest Quality system of human morality based on universal principles. But before we get there, I want to take a quick trip through the history of the universe and see how static quality patterns grow, develop, and eventually give rise to each of the four levels of existence.

Once we have this background context, we'll be able to appreciate just how important Wing Chun is in personal and universal terms.

Sit **Up**

They were on the long bus ride home from their debate tournament, deep in conversation about rights and their origins.

Inevitably this devolved into a discussion about the nature of the universe. Wadded pieces of paper were used to describe the ever-expanding nature of spacetime.

Their small group huddled in the back fell silent as each member got within the infinite void of experience.

Also known as navel gazing.

A significant amount of time passed as each young mind drifted farther and farther into the hypothetical.

He eventually thought of the one member of the debate team who hadn't been able to make it, and how much he would have enjoyed being in on this cosmic scale conversation.

He sat up.

Exactly at the same time as the four other students sat up.

The synchronized movement was uncanny enough to spook them all. Their eyes narrowed. Each wondering who was playing a trick on the other.

"I wish..." he got out before his friend cut him off.

"We all have to promise to tell the truth. We all sat up for a reason, and it feels like there's something special with this. Give your word to total honesty." his friend said.

They all silently nodded.

"OK. What were you going to say?" his friend prompted.

"I was laying there thinking about everything we had talked about, and got lost in there when I thought of Aaron who couldn't make it. I was going to say how much I thought he would have liked to be a part of it."

"What?!" they all said together. "That's exactly what I was thinking! I sat up to say the same thing!"

This was his first experience with synchronicity, and his first peek into the mysteries of connection.

A Quick Tour Through the History of the Universe

Now that we understand how every single object, action, idea, or experience is an expressions of values, we can begin to piece together a coherent approach that can help us understand life on multiple dimensions.

What's fascinating is, every single value pattern you can define is simultaneously its own entity with definite borders, edges, and limits, but also a part of a greater association of value patterns. It's both entirely self sufficient and interconnected with a larger context, which is, itself, a single pattern as well as a part of a yet larger pattern.

One thousand years ago, the sum total of human knowledge had no understanding of aerodynamics, the speed of light, relativity, cryptography, or many thousands of disciplines that are old news to us now. Each total is quickly integrated as part of a new total. Every single domain does this. Every quality pattern is a total in and of itself, and a part of a yet larger total.

Ink is a whole static value pattern we call a letter. A whole letter is part of a word. A whole word is a part of a sentence. A whole sentence is part of a paragraph. A whole paragraph is part of a chapter. A whole chapter is part of a book. A whole book is part of a library. A whole library is part of human knowledge. On and on the patterns go, constantly giving rise to more and more patterns of wholes and parts in an infinite dance of increasing complexity.

What's also interesting is how each expression of Quality tends to maintain its existence in a sort of self-preservation. Pattern B values preconditions A, and as long as preconditions A are maintained, Pattern B will continue to exist, even when its material constituents may differ. Think of the value pattern we call "oxygen." It's composed of eight protons, eight neutrons, and eight electrons. Oxygen does not have to be these eight specific protons; any eight protons will do. Oxygen doesn't need eight specific neutrons; any eight neutrons will do. Oxygen doesn't need eight specific electrons; any eight will do. It's less about the specific parts and more about the pattern that their interrelationship expresses that matters.

Another way to think about it is that an overhand knot is an overhand knot whether it's tied in clothesline, nylon, hemp rope, fishing line, or any other material that can be bent and shaped into the pattern we call 'overhand knot.' Overhand knot will maintain its pattern as long as its preconditions 'left over right, right over left' have been met.

But even while maintaining its unique pattern state of "overhand knot" the value pattern of "knot" is a part of the whole called "rope." This shows us how individual value patterns are constantly accommodating, interacting, and participating with other value patterns at higher and lower levels of association. The knot is in the rope which is a part of the rigging of this boat which is the property of a company which is on a mission, etc etc.

Every value pattern is an expression of its own quality, as well as a part of a "bigger" pattern of value. It maintains its personal identity and group association at the same time. As its preconditions change, so does its pattern and expression of the quality state it finds itself in on an individual/ complete level and a group/part level.

Now, when an individual pattern of quality interacts with another pattern of quality to create a new singular whole, there's often a result that goes beyond anything you could expect from each part on its own. This where the saying, "The whole is more than the sum of its parts" comes from. New characteristics and value patterns are expressed in association with the new preconditions A+B.

The term for this emergent property that goes beyond the effect of each value pattern contributing individually is "synergy." Or, as Buckminster Fuller defined it, "behavior of whole systems unpredicted by the behavior of their parts taken separately." Every single level of value patterns coming together creates synergistic effects that transcend each value pattern's limitations and gives rise to novel capabilities.

A drastic example is to show you how you can study the simple value pattern of oxygen forever, but it will never give you anything you can use to predict the behavior of the person who is currently breathing it. The person is a collection of atoms, molecules, organelles, cells, organs, systems, behaviors, experiences, memories, and thoughts. Each level of value patterns that come together to form a high-value pattern always creates synergies that open new potential beyond the capacity of each lower pattern.

But, everything that goes up must come down. Nothing escapes entropy. Just as value patterns can transcend their limitations in synergistic cooperation, they can also degrade along the same pathway. When the preconditions for the whole value pattern are no longer "good quality," the value pattern will break down to its constituent value patterns. When preconditions for life are no longer met, a person will die, their organs shut down, and the cells die. As the cells die, their organic processes stop, and the whole body decomposes down to molecules. The biochemical molecules no longer have a good quality environment, so they break down to their component elements.

So these fundamental aspects of value patterns are always at play. It's a constant flow of valuing individual quality patterns, adapting to contextual patterns (maintaining interrelation with other quality patterns as part of a whole), synergistic transcendence, and potential for decomposition. These four intercompeting expressions of quality are found at every level, every pattern, and every relationship between them, regardless of physical matter, intellectual, biological, or social dynamics, or any other way you can think to frame it.

So you can see how the whole of the universe is an expression of quality through patterns of value that, due to the miracle of synergy, always transcend their individual limitations and create new value patterns in an infinite dance of the universe. Every time a new value pattern emerges, it moves 'up' in complexity.

Quality patterns are inherently organized by hierarchy.

Every new level incorporates its parts, but creates its own expression of values. This is where the organization of inorganic, biological, social, and intellectual comes from. It's woven into the very fabric of reality itself. There is no way around this process, for it's the process of processes!

Each new value pattern includes its predecessors, but unifies them into a new whole. The new pattern has all of its parts in itself, but not all of itself is in the parts like the person vs. oxygen patterns. The person is an emergent pattern of many lower-quality patterns operating in synergistic concert to give rise to the new higher quality social and intellectual biological specimen.

To put it in literature terms again: all the words

are in the sentence, but the sentence is not in any of the words. When the individual patterns called 'words' are arranged in the new pattern called 'sentence,' each word is oriented in relationship to the higher quality pattern called "meaning." What the sentence means is a functional synergy of the letters and words working together to create the higher-order value pattern of the sentence.

While 'meaning' is a higher-quality value pattern than 'word,' meaning is not beyond words. The higher-order quality patterns are defined by the lower level patterns. Your mind operates on the highest level of quality: intellectual. But it can't wish itself not to be affected by gravity. If you're standing under a falling anvil, I don't care how much you think about it missing you, you're going to be crushed. This is how fundamental quality patterns define the parameters of higher order quality patterns. Low-quality patterns define the *possibilities* of higher-quality value patterns, whereas higher quality value patterns define the *probabilities* of lower-quality value patterns.

An intellectual creature called 'person' can

directly affect the probability of an inorganic piece of iron ore being shaped into (or arranged into a new value pattern that we call) 'a spring' for a car's suspension system, or being forged into a sword.

This is why fundamental levels define the possibilities of higher levels, and higher levels define the probabilities of lower levels.

Fundamental quality patterns like gravity and thermodynamics directly limit the person's possibility of wishing themselves off the Earth (an intellectual quality pattern). This is exactly why pseudoscientific claptrap like "the Secret" is patently wrong. There's no way to violate the fundamental forces of reality. You can only operate within their constraints. No amount of wishing, hoping, or praying is going to do anything in the physical world.

As each level defines and shapes each successive level, we can begin to see it as a trade off between breadth and depth. Lower-quality patterns have great breadth, but little depth.

Higher-quality patterns have great depth, but very narrow breadth.

Quantum particles have near infinite breadth as they're the most fundamental pattern of quality known to man. Many of those quantum particles come together to form subatomic particles like protons. Some form neutrons. Then some of those particles come together to form atoms. Some of those atoms come together to form molecules. Some molecules come together in a way that allows them to reproduce.

The higher the quality pattern, the greater depth it has, and the narrower breadth it has, too. This is simply due to the fact that fewer parts meet the higher bar to qualify as this more complex pattern. If you only had 100 atoms in the universe, there could never be more than 50 molecules. In this example, atoms would have a breadth of 100 and a depth of 1. Molecules would have a breadth of 50, and a depth of 2. There can never be more higher quality patterns than lower quality patterns that comprise it.

More depth means less breadth, but depth can be thought of as capacity for consciousness. Abstract reasoning is an incredibly complex process that is the synergistic quality of millions of sub-value patterns working in concert to even make it feasible. Other creatures seem to display consciousness on a spectrum of complexity. This is why some creatures can solve problems and why a simple amoeba can respond to its environment.

The more complex the creature, the more complex the behaviors it can embody.

But how do you figure out where a particular value pattern sits on the spectrum? Try the thought experiment of getting rid of that pattern. What happens? Whatever depends on that pattern to exist would wink out of existence. Everything below it would continue on just fine.

Get rid of people, and the intellectual world would disappear. Probably culture, too depending on how you define it. But, we know for sure that biology would continue. Molecules would continue. But get rid of organic molecules? All life disappears. Get rid of molecules entirely, and all chemistry disappears. All value patterns above the level of atoms would be impossible.

This is how you can tell whether a pattern is fundamental or significant. High breadth and low depth is fundamental. Great depth and low breadth is not fundamental, but it is highly significant. The higher quality the value pattern, the more value patterns it incorporates, which makes it massively significant to the universe.

This is why Quality is both fundamental and significant! It is the very fabric of patterns of value at every level. The patterns don't exist in a vacuum. They grow, develop, evolve, and create together in a concurrent, interdependent dance of synergy. Lower level quality patterns are constantly interacting with higher level quality patterns, and humans are arguably the only value patterns in the universe that exist as an expression of inorganic, biological, social, and intellectual patterns simultaneously. We are an amalgamation of atoms and elements that reproduce through biological sexual processes moderated through social interactions guided by our intellectual pursuits.

Wavy *Fog*

"That's how you know it's Chi," his instructor said. "Put your forearm on the mirror and use it to rest your other hand on it. That way you can get your palm close to the mirror and see for yourself."

He shrugged and decided to try it for himself.

He put his arm against the mirror and rested his other hand on top as he put his palm close to the mirror's surface.

The glass fogged up, but the top edge was moving back and forth like slow motion fire.

This was the proof his instructor was talking about.

"See," the instructor said on his way by, "if

it was just from the heat of your hand it would just fog up. Since it's waving like that, it's evidence of the energy!"

He remained skeptical of what clearly smacked of Bullshido.

Chapter 3

Mandelbrot Set of Quality

This whole process of iterative value patterns at higher and higher levels of Quality is echoed in the world of fractals, as they are both expressions of the same fundamental truths of the universe. The most famous fractal is the Mandelbrot set, which was the discovery of Benoit Mandelbrot, an American-French-Polish mathematician.

Fractals are geometric shapes created by feeding a number through a relatively simple formula, plotting the result on a graph, and then feeding the result through the same formula, plotting the new result on the graph, and continuing to do so until the final number reaches zero or rockets off into infinity.

Understanding this is the key to understanding how a simple process can create infinite complexity. The process can be simple, but the result can be complex. This is true for first-order effects, an order of magnitude more true for second order effects, and so on down the line to infinity.

Fractals (and our lives) are a recursive process; the input dictates the output, which then becomes the new input to the same formula. The Mandelbrot set is the set of results from running numbers through Mandelbrot's formula, which only relies on addition and multiplication. It has a distinctive appearance, with shapes echoed in a variety of mathematical domains.

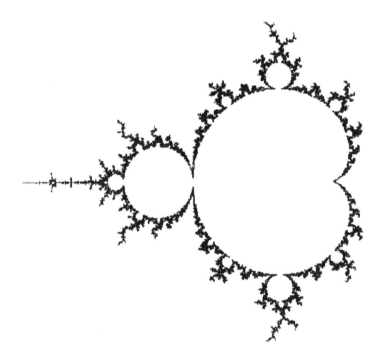

This is what it looks like when you're completely zoomed out. This is the whole thing. The magic happens when you start to zoom in at 10x or 100x.

You'll see this same shape repeated at smaller and smaller scales. The more you zoom in, the more of this same shape you'll see.

The incredible thing about this fractal is that it's infinitely complex in a literal sense. It's not just really complex so we say it's infinite; no, it's really infinite. You could continue plotting numbers for the rest of time, zoom in farther, and still never reach the end of its pattern.

You could enlarge the pattern until the illustration that's a mere 3 inches now spanned the width of the whole known universe, and you still wouldn't reach the end of its complexity. Also, you'd continue to see the same large-scale pattern showing up which you could zoom in on for the rest of eternity without reaching its end.

This is a powerful way to think about Wing Chun. It's fairly simple at first glance, but the deeper you look into it, the more intricate the patterns get. You'll also find the same patterns showing up again and again, and at different scales. This is why I advise a 1x zoom look at the Wing Chun system; a quick overview. Then a 10x zoom at more of the small details. Then you can zoom in 100x to get down to the nitty gritty details.

In a conflict, the person who can handle the higher-magnification zoom will always win. If you can only see the 1x version of an issue and your opponent can see 100x more complexity than you, it means they have an advantage that's two orders of magnitude more powerful than yours. If you can see 1 mile ahead, they can see 100 miles.

This is why your Wing Chun practice is never complete. It's a lifelong exercise of discovering finer- and finer-scale refinements that you can apply to every facet of your life. It's also a recursive relationship. Every choice you make now (input) gives you a certain result (output) which is what you have to work with for the next moment (input).

Each choice becomes a recursive feedback loop that amplifies the quality of the initial input, whether it's good or bad. The sum pattern of your choices defines the shape your life takes.

This is where the adage "how you do anything is how you do everything" comes from. Your small choices create the results that become your big choices. Up and down the patterns repeat until you've run out of options.

Wing Chun is the science of optimizing your decision making formula to create higher and higher-quality results that become better and better options in the next moment, days, weeks, months, and years in a fractal symmetry that expresses at greater and greater complexities.

Breathe *Out*

He knew what it wasn't; it wasn't an out of body experience.

But the thing is, he had no idea what it was, either.

It happened during the couple months in

high school when he studied "Emperor's Long Fist" Kung Fu at the Monday night classes held at the community center, and years before he started experimenting with drugs.

Students were going through a Chi Gung exercise; low horse stance, breathing in conjunction with moving the arms in a particular sequence.

They were all facing the wall covered with a full floor to ceiling mirror. He was watching himself go through the motions, and his mind was on breathing out when the weirdest thing happened.

He was the room.

His identity, the 'he' that he usually identified as, was no longer trapped by his skin. Everything he saw was 'he.'

It was not a dissociative experience; there was no separation or dividing. It was an including, or encompassing experience.

The sensation lasted for several seconds and was completely disorienting.

The ego part of his mind freaked out, understandably, and there was a full body sensation not unlike a lurch, and the 'he' was back to the usual comfortable limit of his skin boundary.

He told the instructor what happened, and got the reply, "Yeah, that kind of weird stuff will happen when you're doing Chi Gung."

He still thought it was probably a brain hiccup, as the mind is prone to error, but that was the birth of his lifelong obsession with discovering where the limits of human existence can be found.

He is still searching.

Moiré Effect

In mathematics, physics, art, and industry a Moiré pattern is a large-scale interference pattern that emerges when two similar patterns with a solid and transparent appearance interact. The effect will not show up if both patterns are exactly the same; they need to be different in terms of repetition, scale, orientation, rotation, or some other change in relationship. The Moiré pattern is a larger expression of the smaller patterns created at the points where they intersect, so you can think of the Moiré pattern as a meta-pattern of sorts.

You can see it in action while driving on the highway. Overpasses commonly have chain link fence on both sides of the bridge. The same diamond-shape fencing is displaced by distance and this is enough of an offset to create the meta-pattern of a larger diamond Moiré Pattern.

The effect is not "real" in the sense that you can touch it, but it's definitely an effect you can see. This is principle is especially powerful in life.

People constantly make different choices using the same thought processes. And, as we see with the world of fractals, even a simple process can yield infinite complexity. Lives are the complex result of using the same decision making processes across greater and greater time scales.

This is fractal nature of life. Choices are Fractal; lessons are Moiré.

Patterns of choices play out at a moment-to-moment time scale, daily time scale, weekly, monthly, and on up until you're fully zoomed out at 1x magnification looking at one lifetime.

When viewed through each time scale, the smaller fractal value patterns interfere with each other, and larger meta-patterns will be readily apparent.

This is a "seeing the forest" moment when you realize seeing each tree individually does nothing, but broad context does everything.

Wake *Up*

3:30am and someone was screaming.

The earth moved and nothing made sense. He woke up to a slow motion nightmare.

"How could you?!" she yelled. "You piece of shit! You've been lying to me!"

She kicked the bed again. Harder.

"Wake up!"

"What?!" he yelled back, not quite awake, but already feeling the shame full-force.

She had found the months of text messages, the inappropriate emails, photos, voicemails.

Everything.

She blamed herself.

She sobbed.

He knew it wasn't her fault. He knew it didn't involve her. It affected her, sure, but it wasn't her responsibility.

He'd gotten married. Gotten soft. Put on weight. Nearly 50 pounds.

She told him point blank, "I don't find you attractive any more."

They hadn't slept together in months.

He had a choice.

Take it as a wake up call and shape up, or blame her for all those damn casseroles and find someone to validate his slide into apathy.

He chose poorly.

And after nearly a year she found out.

They went through marriage counseling, but it was a formality. They each silently agreed to the charade so they could say "we tried everything."

He left with his laptop, books, car, college debt, and guilt. She kept everything else including the friends.

She eventually remarried. To his former good friend, the lawyer.

The void engulfed him.

The Prime Geometry of Nature

This is one of the last pieces of the puzzle we have to put into place before we dive into the world of Wing Chun. Finally we'll have enough context to understand and appreciate the genius of the Wing Chun system for its simplicity, directness, and efficiency at cultivating personal integrity.

For now, however, we will work step by step to wrap our minds around how reality moves from zero to one dimensions[1], one to two dimensions[2], two to three dimensions[3], and then three to four dimensions[4].

But first we have to discuss infinity.

Eureka!

One of the most fundamental issues in all of mathematics is the nature of infinity. It's such a difficult concept because we humans are

---

1   Nothing to Something
2   Length to Area
3   Geometry to Space
4   Space to Spacetime

bounded by our experience and position in life. We have limited reach, literally and metaphorically.

We have a tough time appreciating the vast distances that span our own solar system, let alone the distance between our solar system and the next. We can quantify them with numbers, but fully grasping their meaning is difficult.

Such is the nature of infinity. Or, rather, infinites, plural.

There are essentially two types of infinity: potential and actual.

First, lets deal with potential.

Imagine you're at an auction, and you're bidding for someone who, for all intents and purposes has infinite money. He tells you that you are to outbid the competition at all costs. Never let someone else win the auction. Whatever the bid, you can always bid one more. No matter how long this process goes, you'll always be able to top it, but the total will be definite. It is bounded. The total might be a giant number, but at least it will stop some time. This is the infinity of potential.

No matter what it is now, it could always be more. It has no foreseeable limit in the future, but it's presently bounded.

Actual infinity is just that: real infinity. No beginning or end. Literally infinite, like the number of points along a line; since they have no dimension, their number is literally infinite. That's why mathematicians have a hard time believing it even exists; even in a purely abstract way. Our minds have a tough time appreciating the concept because it's not just big; it's infinite.

It's also an incredibly sophisticated concept; this idea of multiple types of infinities. Infinite is infinite, right? It wasn't until the 19th and 20th centuries that math progressed to the point of being able to differentiate types of infinities.

Or was it?

Plural infinity would be the sole brainchild of the

20th century if it weren't for a small book bought at a Christie's auction in 1998 for $2 million. It was a hymnal from 1229 with even older roots. The hymnal was actually a palimpsest; a book made from a previous book.

Back in those days materials were scarce, and incredibly valuable. Old books that weren't any use to anyone were dismantled, scrubbed clean, and the vellum was made ready to be turned into a holy book.

But this particular palimpsest wasn't made from just any old book; it was a priceless treasure. It was made from the only surviving copy of a book written by Archimedes; the Greek mathematician and arguably the most intelligent person in the history of human beings.

This is the guy who famously ran through the streets naked after his bath overflowed when he sat down in it. He shouted "Eureka!" because he figured out how to quantify density as a function of weight and volume. His fundamental insight was he could measure an object's volume by measuring how much water that object would displace.

Archimedes also created techniques that solved mathematical problems which wouldn't be addressed again until the creation of Calculus in mid-17th century by Isaac Newton and Gottfried Leibniz. Archimedes also calculated the value of pi to four decimal points which is a staggering achievement.

Consider this: if you were trying to figure out how much fencing you'd need to enclose a swimming pool with a 100 meter radius, and used pi calculated to one more decimal point than Archimedes used, you'd be just half a millimeter short. You'd be off by less than the width of a handsaw blade. This is the precision that Archimedes could measure, quantify, and calculate 300 years before Jesus was born.

But this was all old news. The Archimedes Palimpsest revealed unbelievable insights.

Archimedes had already considered multiple

infinities 2,000 years before the finest mathematicians in the world came up with the concept, and this book was the only proof in the world.

Archimedes conceptualized several types of potential infinities with a thought experiment. Imagine a plane with real infinity; perfectly flat, and extending forever. This is the first infinity. Now, put points on the plane. No matter how many points you populate it with, you can always add more. This is the second infinity. Now, draw a straight line connecting any two points. How many lines could you draw that satisfy this constraint? This is the third infinity. How many curved lines could you draw connecting any two points? Infinite curved lines for just those two points; and there are infinite numbers of two points that you could draw infinite numbers of curves to connect them with!

This is how you get from nothing to something.

The infinite plane is perfectly flat, with no dimension. It's pure abstraction, or functionally 'zero.' So is a point. In geometry, a point is simply a location. It has no length, width, or depth to it. It's represented by a dot, even though a dot is misleading because it's 'something.' But, for now, understand that we're dealing with a perfectly abstract point with no dimension.

When you put a second dot on the same plane as the first and draw a line between the two you have created the first dimension: length.

Place a third point on the same plane as the first two, but make sure it doesn't touch the line drawn between them, nor possibly touched if the line is extended past the first two.

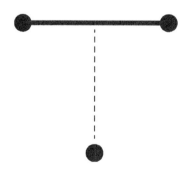

This is the second dimension: width.

If you connect the three points, you create the simplest closed shape possible when using straight lines; the triangle.

This is the beginning of structure: the domain of area. The triangle is incredibly strong, stable, and efficient. An equilateral triangle is especially elegant; all three sides (or lines) are the same length, and the total measure of the angles created by them are all 180°.

It doesn't matter what the real length of the sides are; their ratio always stays the same. This is the infinity of trigonometry. Add the interior angles of a triangle and they will always total 180°, but it's only an equilateral triangle that is evenly divided into three 60° angles.

In order to talk about the third dimension, volume, we're going to leave the world of pure mathematical abstractions, and think more literally with a bar bet you can use to get yourself free drinks from your friends.

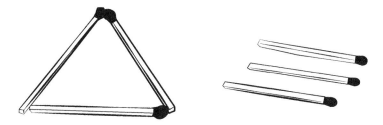

Put six toothpicks or matches on the table, and tell your friend that the point of the game is to arrange them in such a way they make four equilateral triangles. No bending, breaking, or dismantling allowed. They have to stay intact and arranged to form four triangles with equal length sides.

You'll watch your friends make two equilateral triangles on the table top, and then declare your challenge to be impossible. Try not to smile at their limited imagination. See, the answer lies in working in three dimensions.

Use three matches to make an equilateral triangle on the table, and then lean the tips of the other three against each other like a tee-pee to make a pyramid shape called a tetrahedron.

This shape, the tetrahedron, is a remarkable shape worth examining. Its secrets are the building blocks of Wing Chun.

It has four equilateral triangle faces, four vertex corners, six straight edges, and a total of 720 degrees[5]. It's perfectly symmetrical. No matter which way it is oriented, it still maintains balance and the central axis is in the same place.

It is also the simplest structure in three dimensional space with volume. There's an

---

5   Three 60° angles per triangle times four triangles equals 720° total. 4(3x60)=720

inside and an outside; a positive tetrahedron and a negative tetrahedron, if you will. It's the simplest expression of micro and macro cosmic scales, too.

Now, imagine you had a tetrahedron along with a cube, a dodecahedron, and whatever other shape you can imagine and they're all made out of cheese. Take a cheese slicer, and cut off one of their faces to make a slice that's perfectly uniform in depth.

Now, what remains of every shape would be lopsided by the amount you cut away. . . except the tetrahedron. It would still be perfectly symmetrical, no matter which way it's oriented.

Another way of putting it is if you move a face to its opposite vertex, the lengths of the edges get smaller at a constant velocity. Additionally, the area of each face gets smaller at velocity squared, and the volume of the tetrahedron gets smaller at velocity cubed with a simple elegance.

Since we know that the length, area, and volume

change in the same velocity across dimensions (single power, squared, and cubed), then they will all reach 0 at the same time, too.

Which means, you could theoretically have a zero-dimension tetrahedron. What that looks like is the intersection of four planes at the same angles as the sides of the tetrahedron.

It's like your front/back and left/right symmetrical planes were crossing at a single point. Which happens at the balance point of all bodies; a truth verified by Archimedes. In martial arts this balance point is often called the "dan tien" which is loosely translated as "energy center."

The tetrahedron is the simplest transition from infinite to bounded space, and there's proof.

Imagine you're making a bear skin rug which means you want to translate the 3 dimensional shape of the bear into a simple flat geometric plane through a process that's basically a weird sort of reverse origami.

Every place there's a rise in the skin you'll cut

a relief from the edge of the skin to the center point of the rise. As the skin flattens out, the place where you cut it will open up at an angle.

Once the skin is flattened out, you can measure the angles of the relief cuts, and you'll find they total 720.

Every single time, and this is true for any bounded shape. Beach ball, banana peel, or light bulb it doesn't matter. Any closed 3 Dimensional shape will flatten out if 720° are added to it.

The reverse is also true.

You can take a flat piece of paper (the flat geometric plane of infinity), cut sections out of it to create a closed shape, measure the angles of the pieces you cut away from the shape, and you'll see they always total 720°.

This means that the difference between infinity and bounded space is exactly one tetrahedron.

It gets weirder.

Happy *Birthday*

It was her birthday, and he was going to make it special.

They woke up late, had a lazy mid-afternoon breakfast, and enjoyed a too-long shower together that involved getting dirty. Twice. It was her birthday after all.

High on feel-good endorphins they got dressed and decided it was time to go to the movies. Holding hands they walked out into the blinding Texas summer when his stomach dropped.

"Where's my car?" he thought. "It was parked. right. there. FUCK."

But he already knew. He didn't know where, exactly, it was but he knew why it was gone.

They found it.

It had been repossessed.

For months he had been careful. His name wasn't on the apartment's lease. Left no forwarding address. Nobody knew where to find him. And it had worked, in a manner of speaking.

Until her birthday.

The rest of the day was spent on hold. Waiting for a customer service rep to help you, because your call is very important to us.

Wheeling and dealing, convincing the woman on the other end of the line that he needed the car to get to his next gig where he could afford to catch up on his payments.

He'd already driven it all over the country, so they could auction it off and get nothing for it, or add penalties to the back end of the loan and squeeze more money out of him.

They went for it. They were returning his car after he pays the towing fees.

He talked his way out of another tight spot.

For awhile.

Unsurprisingly the relationship deteriorated. She eventually cheated on him. Bragged about all the things she did with the other guy that she never did with a loser like him.

His life was in shambles.

Chapter **6**

Action/Reaction

We've already touched on this idea from the standpoint of "B values preconditions A," so causality is merely a linguistic trick that helps us smooth over the clunky nature of what's really going on, but now we're going to come at causality, or "action/reaction" from another angle.

Cause and effect happen fast enough to be essentially instantaneous, and for most of human history, it hasn't even been a distinction worth making because it's so obvious. But, since humans figured out the speed of light, we've known that there is no such thing as instant; there's an upper speed limit built into the very fabric of the universe.

Experience is bounded by three dimensions. First there's an action. Most know about the second dimension of experience; the reaction from Newton's Third Law of Motion which states, "For every action, there is an equal and opposite reaction." What he left out, however, is the situation created from the action and reaction playing out. This is the third dimension: the resultant.

Every action is essentially an expression of energy in one form or another, and every energy event is a vector: speed **+** direction. Basically it's a line of an energy event taking place in a particular direction.

The line's momentum is velocity **x** mass of the thing moving over a given duration with respect to the angle of the observer (your frame of reference).

These lines don't extend into infinity; we know they're bounded because we understand that the speed of light is not infinite either. These vectors are measurable with a beginning and an end. Every action (energy vector) is coupled with its reaction and its resultant, which are themselves, distinct.

This can be expressed as three lines extending at their own vectors, but never in 180° alignment due to the nature of precession: the effect of a body's motion on another body's motion.

The whole universe is an interwoven pattern of dynamic quality pattern wholes and parts of wholes in motion on a variety of scales and distances. This is why all effects are precessional. They will curve and bend in directions you may not expect because it's essentially impossible to understand the sum total of the vectors involved.

This is why a relatively straightforward situation can rapidly spiral out of control.

Think about the orbits of the planets around the sun. The force of gravity operates along a straight line between the centers of mass of the two (or more) bodies in motion. Theoretically, the Earth should plunge straight into the heart of the Sun, but it doesn't.

Why?

Because it has enough of its own momentum and

rotational inertia that when the straightforward force of the sun's gravity acts on it, the resultant situation is such that the Earth is constantly moving at a perpendicular vector to the line of attraction.

Taking all this into account gets us back to Action / Reaction / Resultant. They always form a three-part shape. They form a helix, a zig-zag, a Z shape, or a triangle, but never a straight line.

The helix shape is particularly interesting, and you can play with it yourself if you get pipe cleaners. Use two colors like white and black, and bend them to create two equilateral triangles. Orient them so the corner where the ends meet is at 12 o'clock. On the white triangle, bend the left section up until each end is about one segment's length distance away from each other. On the black, do the same to the right segment.

Play with them long enough and you'll realize the two shapes can be oriented together to create a tetrahedron!

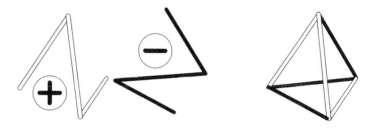

What happens if you tried again but lifted the left segment on both of the shapes? They'll never fit together. The tetrahedron is only possible when there's one 'positive' and one 'negative' helix.

In this way we can understand the open triangular spiral, or helix, as action / reaction / resultant and it becomes half of a bounded shape, structure, or in other terms the simplest form of reality. Through an association of positive and negative helix patterns we can see that the tetrahedron is the volumetric unit of bounded reality as defined from infinity.

From the world of geometry, cause/effect/ resultant, energy, and physics, we see how the whole universe is a metapattern of tetrahedron associations of yin/yang, positive/negative, up/ down, and all other infinite dualities unfolding simultaneously along multiple dimensions of dynamic quality patterns.

First *Introductions*

He was helping run a science conference in Vegas put on by his mentor; a world famous critical thinker.

The two of them were having breakfast at the casino's diner when someone who clearly knew his mentor walked up.

"Ah," his mentor said to him, "here's someone you should know. He's a Kung Fu master."

With his previous experience dabbling in bullshido, he figured meeting a Kung Fu man at a science conference probably meant that this was the best chance he was going to get to learn Kung Fu from someone who wasn't going to waste his time with Chi fog.

He was right; that single meal changed his life.

Chapter 7

Tensegrity

The word "tensegrity" is a mashup of the words "tension" and "integrity" created by Buckminster Fuller, and the idea points to a structure's stability resulting from the tension between components that resist tension[1] and components that resist compression[2].

Tension components, or members, pull away from a center like a length of rope does. As the two ends are pulled away from each other, the rope becomes taut and its thickness is decreased everywhere along its entire length which is a resultant perpendicular to the initial direction of force.

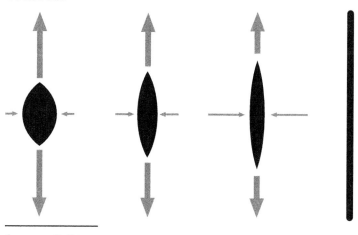

---

1   Pulling
2   Pushing

Compression members, like straight-sided columns, resist pushing towards a center. If it is loaded with a heavy enough weight at its top, the column can start to bulge and distort from the perfectly straight edges into a subtly bowed cigar shape.

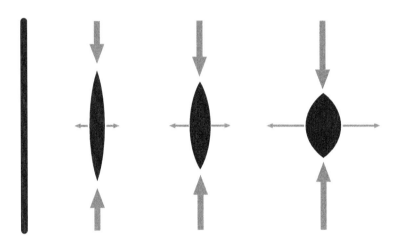

The vertical compression applies tension horizontally due to internal stresses of the structure. Even if the results are not visible to the naked eye, the forces are at work.

If a compression member is too long, weak, and narrow, however, it will simply bend and break into at least two shorter members. If a tension member is too brittle, it will simply snap into two or more shorter tension members.

An ideal tension member is highly resilient to pulling along its vertical axis, and distributes small amounts of compression forces along its horizontal axis. An ideal compression member resists pushing along its length, and distributes tension along its horizontal axis. As one force is at high tide in the appropriate member[3], its complement is at low tide; which is another way of explaining the forces of Yin and Yang.

The tendency for a material to distribute force perpendicular to its structure is a function of precession; just like what causes the three-part energy event of action, reaction, and resultant to create a helix shape instead of a straight line. And depending on what materials it's made of and how they are integrated, a system can withstand both forces of tension and compression in a resilient manner. This would be a tensegrity structure.

---

3   Compression is high tide in a column, with tension at low tide. Tension is at high tide in a rope, or cable, and compression is at low tide.

Suspension bridges, like the Golden Gate Bridge, get their strength as a function of tensegrity. Their I-beams are the compression-resisting components, and their cables are the tension-resisting components. Together, they distribute incredible forces across the entire structure instead of at the point where the load meets the bridge.

Another example would be a camping tent. The rigid poles give the fabric a frame to hang on, and the lines staked to the ground apply tension to the whole structure so it doesn't collapse in on itself. This would be considered a tensegrity structure.

Here's another way to put it. Imagine a tetrahedron that is big enough to sit on a coffee table. Each of its six sides are made out of hollow PVC pipe and bungee cords run through the length of the pipes to connect them all together. The bungee provides the tension, and the pipes provide the resistance to the compression. The result is a springy structure that yields against pressure, but bounces right back while remaining highly static.

The human body is a tensegrity structure. Our bones are the compression members and our muscles are the tension members. Unlike a static pipe-and-bungee tetrahedron, a body is a high Quality, dynamic tensegrity structure. It can bend, twist, push, pull, crawl, walk, run, jump, tumble, vault, and perform thousands of other complex actions all thanks to the interplay of the parts that resist pulling and the parts that resist pushing.

Wing Chun is the science of how all these concepts work together to maintain your physical, mental, emotional, and spiritual[4] integrity.

Universe *Unfolding*

"What the hell was that?!" he said.

"What was what," his instructor asked.

---

4   I'm not talking about spirit in a religious sense. I'm talking about it as the root meaning of "inspire" as a breath for life, enthusiasm, etc. Something distinctly missing from the postmodern "nothing means anything" proponents. With Wing Chun, you'll discover you have a life worth living.

It was late in the evening, and they had been grappling in what amounted to his instructor's living room.

"I don't know. You kept getting me into all these submissions, and then a way out would open up, and I'd take it. But then, my whole body experienced, or saw, I don't know how to put it; my whole body saw a bunch of triangles that wrapped around to form a sort of donut shape that folds in on itself.

Each facet could unfold in a variety of directions, and we were working our way through different pathways. What the hell is that all about?!"

"Now you get it," his instructor said. "That's the shape of Kung Fu.
You now know it deep in your body. You now embody Kung Fu.

That's pure Wing Chun."

Chapter **8**

What Is Kung Fu?
The Prime Lethal Geometry

At a 1x magnification Wing Chun is a Southern Chinese Kung Fu system specializing in close range combat. At higher magnifications, it becomes so much more.

Originally Kung Fu didn't mean 'lots of screaming while punching and kicking.' The term Kung Fu translates as a high skill level that is only attainable through hard work and time spent cultivating the craft. It points to the learning and perfecting of one's skills in mind and body rather than applying to what, specifically, is being trained.

A gardener can have Kung Fu. A potter can have Kung Fu. A musician can have Kung Fu. Anyone can have Kung Fu if they dedicate their life to improving their skill and working diligently at cultivating their abilities.

Recently it has come to mean punching and kicking because fewer people are invested in cultivating personal integrity on the physical and metaphysical dimensions.

This is a bit disingenuous, though.

Kung Fu is not just knowing how to fight. It's more about self defense on all levels, which is a subtle, yet important distinction. You are not attacking. It's not called "attacking others." It's "defending self."

It's learning how to keep yourself safe against someone who intends to do you harm. You are not the aggressor. Someone is attacking you, and you should know what to do about it.

Eventually you learn how to impose your will on others, but it all begins by learning how to keep someone else from imposing their will on you first physically and then in more abstract ways.

The same confidence born from being able to protect oneself physically will naturally percolate up from the inorganic and biological levels of Quality to the social and intellectual levels of your life.

There seem to be just as many styles of Kung Fu as people to practice them, and Wing Chun is a type of Kung Fu, but it is demonstrably the highest Quality at cultivating personal integrity on every level. It gets you the most results with the least amount of effort, just like how the universe chooses to allocate its resources.

We'll dive into how it is built on the rock solid principles of Quality, fractal unfolding, and prime geometry of the tetrahedron, but first. . .

Dance *Party*

He stopped in Phoenix to see a friend.

He'd known her for awhile, and when he arrived she told him that there was a party that one of her former roommates was throwing, and she had totally forgotten that it was the same weekend that he was visiting; would he mind coming along?

"Just an appearance, and then we can leave!" *she promised.*

The music was too loud, the light was too low, and there were too many people. It was exactly the type of place he never visits but he was happy to have a break while on tour.

The group was in a VIP section that was up on a step about 6 to 8 inches higher than the dance floor. She was facing the group, and he was on the edge of the platform right behind her facing the same way.

A guy who was about 6 inches taller than he was (even while standing on riser), walked up and put his arm around her shoulder; cutting him out of the group.

He knew that she wasn't expecting any other friends, and the demeanor of the guy's body language told him that he definitely wasn't a friend.
He reached out, took hold of the guy's arm, pulled it off her shoulder, and made sure to

maintain contact as he pointed in the opposite direction.

"Get fucked!" he shouted over the music.

He could tell by the way the guy didn't turn to face him that he wasn't trained in any martial art. He stayed facing forward and allowed his right arm to be held behind him. What the stranger also didn't know was this connection allowed him to instantly feel an attack coming if it was going to happen.

"Hey, I was just…" the stranger got out before he was cut off.

"I don't give a shit what you think you were doing. Get fucked." he said, leaning in. Still in control of the arm.

He could see the wheels turning in the man's alcohol-soaked mind as he did the math.

"Is this girl worth it?"

The stranger eventually came to the conclusion of his cost-to-benefit ratio analysis, and decided against continuing.

He slowly backed away, and walked off into the crowd.

The stranger had blatantly violated his friend's personal space, so he had snapped into action without even thinking of it. He physically engaged the man who was substantially bigger than he was, but he maintained control literally and figuratively through the entire encounter.

She never noticed anything had happened.

Chapter 9

Quick History

It's thousands of years ago, and you live in a village. There's some tension with neighboring villages, and fighting breaks out occasionally. You're the best fighter around, and you miraculously live to see old age.

You're too long in the tooth to be involved in the next breakout of violence, so you're tasked with explaining how you managed to fight so well and teach the next crop of fighters how to make it back home. You're encoding your Dynamic Quality skills into Static Quality patterns that the next generation can benefit from.

You haven't really thought about what made you such a good fighter; you just were one. Now, you have to go from doer to teacher which is an especially difficult transition. This is why Bernard Shaw's maxim, "He who can, does. He who cannot, teaches," is a bit disingenuous. You do the best you can so you explain your skills by using metaphors and analogy.

"I fight with the ferocity of a tiger, the flexibility of a snake, and the quickness of a rabbit. Study those animals, and bring their spirit to your training!"

As an educational strategy, it works reasonably well. More of your students become old fighters themselves who teach new generations of fighters who continue the tradition on down the line. Each generation keeps the knowledge that's most effective, drops what doesn't work, and each revision becomes more efficient.

And this process is happening in every village, every generation.

This is the ruthless evolution of combat.

When fighters from two styles encounter each other, those who are most efficient and effective overcome those who aren't. This leaves the victor to pass the more useful knowledge to the next generation. The ineffective style is weeded out of the martial arts genepool.

There's intense real-world pressure on these skills to work. Over thousands of years each army and its warriors get more and more proficient at the killing arts. Their training strategies, their concepts, and their ways of thinking about combat get ever more elegant.

And then guns come on the scene.

No longer do you need to spend years getting comfortable with close-quarters combat; you can learn how to point the gun 'that way' and pull the trigger. No matter how well trained the Kung Fu master, he's not going to dodge the bullet.

In the 1900's there was a Chinese uprising called the Boxer[1] Rebellion, which was motivated by nationalist sentiments. The ensuing chaos decimated the institutional Kung Fu genepool.

Many masters who resented outside influences and missionaries moving into China were convinced they were immune to foreign

---

1   The Westernized term for Chinese Kung Fu practitioners.

weapons and moved to push them out by direct conflict. Unfortunately for the Kung Fu masters, Chinese leadership was aligned with the interests (and money) of the foreign forces, so the uprising was put down.

Over the next several decades[2] there was the fall of the Qing dynasty, a Japanese invasion, and a Chinese civil war. This turbulence led to the proliferation of training manuals and books published by martial artists who saw it as their duty to teach their fellow countrymen how to defend themselves.

But the Chinese Cultural Revolution[3] led to harsh regulations by the People's Republic of China on the practice of martial arts in order to bring them under the umbrella of the Maoist revolutionary doctrine.

It's due to this warfare, fighting, and continual revolution that many martial artists preferred to remain unknown. Better to keep one's skills secret and survive than to make yourself popular

2   1912-1949

3   1969–1976

and the target of the government's attention.

This is why relatively little is known for certain about the origins of Wing Chun, specifically. Much of its history was maintained solely through verbal transmission, and the teaching of traditions that were not part of the state-sanctioned varieties was done behind closed doors.

The earliest mention of Wing Chun, however, is from the 1850s in reference to practitioners who were part of the "Red Boat Opera." They were a troupe of entertainers who traveled up and down the rivers of China entertaining people, following the tradition of itinerant performers that seems to span all cultures.

However Wing Chun was created and maintained, how it exists today is a testament to its simplicity. Its creators had studied the principles that govern combat and distilled those concepts into simple, practical movements that could be learned quickly and immediately put into practice.

They were geniuses of the highest order and their wisdom for and insight to Quality cannot be overstated.

By the end of this book, hopefully you'll be able to appreciate how they were able to pack so much into so little.

There's no reason to wait years to learn high level techniques and black belt concepts. In Wing Chun, you're encoding those principles directly into your body from day one.

You then spend a lifetime discovering what your body has already learned through your daily practice of the Wing Chun forms.

Millions *Watching*

He was moments away from walking out on stage in front of four celebrity judges, a theater of 2,000 people, and millions of people watching on tv at home.

He was freaking out.

It had been an all day affair of interviews, behind the scene segments, practice, tech rehearsals, paperwork, and sheer nerves. Enduring hours of such grueling emotional highs and anxiety was going to take its toll.

But it was all for this moment.

The producers had told him he was up in five minutes and suddenly it was real. He was about to have a once in a lifetime chance, and he needed to nail it.

He needed to calm down.

He did the only thing he knew to do. Kung Fu.

He walked off to the side and started from the beginning. He faced the wall, took three deep breaths, and began the first form. He moved slowly. Focused on each movement. Each transition. Each posture had his total focus.

His breathing evened out.

He felt grounded.

"One minute!" the producer said into a headset.

He was ready.

He walked over to his mark, peeked out at the audience and the massive opportunity before him, and he smiled.

"This is what I do. This is what I'm here to do. I love this." he thought to himself as he heard someone say, "You're up! Break a leg!"

And he stepped into the spotlight.

Chapter **10**

Wing Chun: The System

Think of Wing Chun like the DNA of self defense: incredibly simple components that fit together to create compact structure that can unfold to near-infinite complexity.

Wing Chun is a system composed of just six forms[1]. These forms are a choreographed sequence of postures and movements, much like a prescribed yoga flow. The difference here is if someone pushed you off the mat, you'd know what to do about it.

Each form has a very specific purpose and internal logic to it that builds off the previous forms. This is why learning the second form will be meaningless unless you've successfully absorbed and embodied the principles of the first. The second builds on the first. The third builds on the first and second, and so on.

We'll spend time with each form's guiding principles in sequence. But, for now, understand

---

1   Echoing the six lines of connection in a tetrahedron which forms the simplest enclosed shape in nature.

that there's another similarity that Wing Chun shares with DNA: it's all built off four components.

Wing Chun's DNA

Just as DNA is only G, C, T, and A, Wing Chun is four components: Chi Gung, Chi Sau, Chi Gerk, and Chin Na. Let's look at each in turn.

Chi Gung

Chi Gung[2] is often considered to be a 'healing arts method of breathing' and is full of pseudoscience. Look on MeetUp.com and you'll see Chi Gung groups everywhere promising some mix of Tai Chi and weird breathing exercises. What most Chi Gung practitioners don't understand is Chi Gung is not a solitary practice; it's part of the larger Kung Fu picture.

Chi Gung isn't simply breathing exercises, though they are a part of it; it's also a method of cultivating whole-body strength and developing physical resilience. Think about doing burpees until you're absolutely sucking wind, and you have the right idea. Chi Gung is basically conditioning

---

2   Often spelled Qigong; it's the same thing.

your body's respiratory and circulatory systems through intense bodyweight exercises.

The breath is the only automatic system you can consciously control, so a breathing practice is the bridge between conscious and unconscious motor functions. By controlling your breath, you can reach the rest of your body's supposedly unreachable automatic systems.

If you want to see the incredible power that Chi Gung has to directly affect your body, look up Wim Hof. He's known as the Ice Man for his spectacular endurance feats with extreme cold. He's also climbed Mt. Everest to 22,000 feet in just shoes and shorts. Also, he demonstrated how he can directly affect the autonomic nervous system by regulating his breathing to overcome an endotoxin he was injected with. This particular endotoxin typically induces violent symptoms, but none manifested in him during the test. To ensure he's not a genetic fluke, he taught his method to ten volunteers over the course of a week who were then, themselves, injected with the endotoxin. None of his students showed any effect, either.

What he taught them is an old Chi Gung exercise that he has branded "The Wim Hof Method." Sounds made up, but he's been tested again and again in rigorous experiments, and he always comes out the other side vindicated. Such is the power of effective breathing.

Each Wing Chun form can be practiced with an emphasis on Chi Gung if you want to cultivate your own superhuman powers like Wim.

Chi Sau

It's an idea, a formal exercise, and a skill all wrapped up into one term which makes it very confusing. Basically think of it as the idea of "sensitivity." It absolutely is not weakness, brittleness, reactiveness, or fragility.

Think about a .50 caliber rifle with a hair trigger. The trigger is very sensitive to pressure, but what happens when it's pulled is anything but weak.

This is the idea of Chi Sau: the power of a massive

explosion held back by the world's most sensitive tripwire.

As a Kung Fu master you have to be incredibly sensitive to the intention and actions of your opponent. The more sensitive you are, the sooner you can perceive what they're trying to do to you, which means you have more time to respond.

You must be powerful and sensitive.

Wing Chun has a built-in practice exercise called Chi Sau where two practitioners make contact with their forearms, and then try to find openings in each other's guard. It's a practice designed to cultivate physical sensitivity and proprioceptive awareness of an opponent's movements.

Chi Gerk

A building is only as strong as its foundation; likewise, your punches and techniques are only as strong as your legs and base supporting them. Movement is freedom, and if you don't know how to move, you won't survive.

Chi Gerk can be thought of as Chi Sau for your legs, in addition to teaching you how to kick, trip an opponent, move in and out of striking range, etc. Instead of dealing with a punch or arm technique, a smart fighter can attack the base and neutralize their opponent from the ground up. If you're able to break someone's balance, they cannot do anything until they've righted themselves.

Motto: "Never skip leg day."

Chin Na

This is the art of seizing and controlling: bone breaks, joint locks, submission holds, limb trapping, etc. Essentially it's forcing joints to bend in directions they're not intended to bend. No matter how big someone's muscles, their joints are equally vulnerable. Most of these techniques are banned in UFC, Bellator, and other combat sports for the permanent damage they tend to inflict. That's why it is good to remember that this is training for life or death situations. We're not advocating for the playful hurting of others!

Many of the wrist grabs and techniques came from the time when you had to physically apprehend someone to arrest them or to prevent someone from reaching for their sword and drawing it. If you were able to grab their wrist, you might delay them long enough to pull your own sword and finish the confrontation.

It also encompasses directly manipulating the clothes an opponent is wearing to control their movements, attacking muscles, tendon connections[3], dislocations, air & blood chokes, or inflicting nerve damage to impair a limb.

Submission holds like triangles, figure fours, kimuras, arm bars, etc. can often be upgraded to a bone break with a sharp impulse, quick POP, or twist. Think of Chin Na techniques as lying on a continuous spectrum between holding on one end and breaking on the other instead of being distinctly separate categories.

---

3   Like the infamous "monkey steals the peaches" technique that works fairly well against male opponents.

A thorough knowledge of Chin Na techniques and principles can mean the difference between panicking when someone grabs you, and silently thanking them for offering you their limb for you to control.

Eventually, Chin Na skills transcend taking advantage of opportunities as they present themselves and eventually lead to planning ahead and making opportunities happen.

Takeaway

As we look into each of the six forms that compose the Wing Chun system, you'll be exposed to these four elements, and you should remember how the simple building blocks of DNA can build complexity through an infinitely exponential fractal pattern of unfolding.

Move *Out*

He let his girlfriend of three years borrow his car for a girl's night out on the city with some of her co-workers. She let him know what neighborhood they'd be in, and to expect her back around midnight.

She said she wasn't going to party too hard.

3:30am he gets the call.

Sounds like she's outside. She's not making sense. Pretty sure he hears her vomiting.

He makes out one word. Alone.

"Don't move. Stay right where you are. I'm coming to get you." he says as he hangs up.

He's deeply upset at this point, but holds out hope that things aren't as bad as they seem. He chooses to focus on the thing that matters: get her home.

How?

She has the car, so he decides to ride his bike. It's five miles away, but he won't have to pay the cab fare while it drives up and down the streets until he finds the needle in the haystack.

It's a popular part of town for late nights, you see.

He spends nearly an hour riding up and down the main roads in the hipster part of town where she told him she would be. Frantically looking at every person, hoping to find her.

He finds his car, first.

A wheel parked up on the sidewalk.

"So she was driving drunk," he thinks.

He notices the passenger door is open, and she's sitting with her feet on the sidewalk, her body leaning out. There's a puddle at her feet. She's passed out.

He gently wakes her up, and she smiles at him. He gets the keys, and puts his bike in the back.

"I'm happy to see you," she says.

He drives home and helps her up the stairs, gets her cleaned up, and into bed where she promptly passes out again.

Her phone is blowing up.

He didn't want her coworkers to worry about her, call the police, and have them show up to the apartment when she's already home safely. He decides to text them back on her behalf. He unlocks the phone.

There are a string of texts going back weeks:

"Thanks for inviting me out."

"I had a lot of fun."

"So glad we got to meet up."

"You're an amazing kisser."

"That was better than I expected."

It was a guy's name she had never mentioned before.

He feels like kicking the bed to wake her up, and screaming at her. He thinks back all those years when he was on the other side of this equation and laughs at the irony.

He lets her sleep.

The next morning he makes them both coffee and he asks her how the night went.
She's embarrassed. She says she's ashamed he saw her like that. But was good to spend some quality time with her girlfriends. They danced. They had fun. They had too many shots, though.

But that was it.

"Anything else happen?" he asks.

She says no.
He takes a deep breath in.

He starts by explaining how driving his car drunk is unacceptable. She could have killed someone, totaled it, or gotten it impounded by parking with its wheels on the sidewalk.

She nods. Accepting the lecture.

A long pause.

"I'm going to need you to move out." he says flatly.

Her eyes don't move from her coffee.

He continues to explain how he can take almost anything, but he can't take being lied to.

He tells her about finding the text messages.

She breaks down. She starts sobbing. She tells him it was assault.

His heart breaks.

The room is perfectly still as they both sit there in the silence that stretches forever between two heartbroken lovers.

He chooses his words very carefully.

"That is a separate issue from you lying to me about your intentions yesterday morning. This is a bigger conversation than just last night. You looked me in the eye and lied to me about what you were going to do. I sincerely hope you get the help you need to resolve the effects of the choices you made last night, but I can't be a part of it. "

It's the single most difficult moment of his life.

It's the most difficult boundary he's ever had to create.

Chapter 11

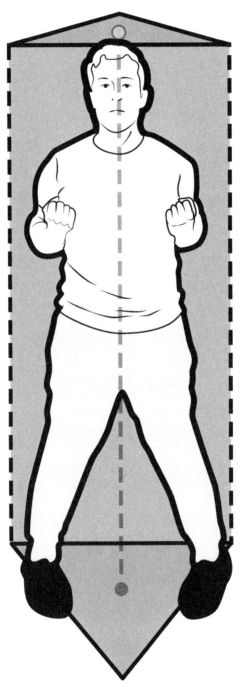

Wing Chun Concepts

Centerline

Most creatures are symmetrical along their center axis, and I call this vertical line of symmetry the Static Centerline. Most of vital organs are placed down the Static Centerline; making this the most vulnerable area[1]. For humans, this means you want to pay special attention to protecting it; a single strike to any number of your Static Centerline areas could mean game over.

Further, the most efficient way to strike your opponent is straight to their Static Centerline. Think about pushing someone's shoulder versus in the middle of their chest. Pushing their shoulder would likely just turn them whereas pushing their chest would move them back.

But what if you're facing your opponent, but standing next to his left arm instead of right in front of him? This is where the concept of

---

1   Your eyes, nose, throat, solar plexus, stomach, and groin are prime examples of this.

the Dynamic Centerline comes in. The Dynamic Centerline is an imaginary line drawn between your Static Centerline and your opponent's Static Centerline. This is the shortest, most direct route between you two. If you're both standing facing each other, your Static and Dynamic Centerlines would be aligned.

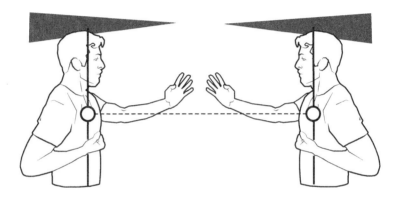

The dotted line represents the Dynamic Centerline.

As you move around your opponent the ideal situation would be to keep your Static Centerline aligned with the Dynamic Centerline while ensuring your opponent's Static Centerline is not aligned with the Dynamic Centerline.

Whoever controls the Dynamic Centerline controls the situation because they can travel

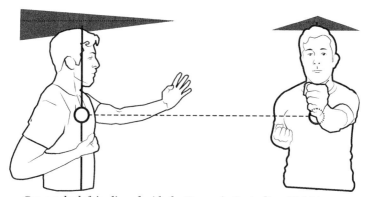

Guy on the left is aligned with the Dynamic Centerline. Right is not.

along the shortest route between the two points, but the other person would have to go around.

This is the longer route, which means it's the slower option. In the world of a violent encounter, slow is dead.

It's the simple fact that a straight line is the shortest distance between two points that informs most of the Wing Chun strategy. Many of the postures focus on keeping your limbs as close to your Static Centerline as possible, and applying them in alignment with the Dynamic Centerline. It also doesn't matter if the structure is intended for attack or defense; occupy the center and the other person will be deflected.

Unfold the Dynamic Centerline concept a little bit, and you'll quickly realize you should apply the closest tool to the closest target. This is why most of the Wing Chun kicks aren't applied any higher than the waist. It wouldn't make sense to punch someone's shin, so why would you kick their head? The higher you kick, the less balanced you will be. That leads us to the next concept.

Balance

What's happening when someone is walking? They're not placing one foot in front of the other while maintaining balance the whole time. They're actually falling forward, and catching themselves with each step.

This is why the smallest trip can lead to the biggest fall.

Consequently, Wing Chun prioritizes a peculiar shuffle step to move around. If at any point during the shuffle either of the feet encounter an obstruction, movement can be stopped immediately. This makes it very difficult for an opponent to trip the Wing Chun practitioner.

Balance is also why Wing Chun never uses techniques that require throwing the whole body behind them like a wild haymaker or high kick. If you over commit and the technique misses, you've gambled too much on a single all-or-nothing effort.

Further, it is very difficult to push or pull someone who knows how to maintain their balance. This makes the Wing Chun practitioner very difficult to control and powerful at any range.

Power is a function of structure, alignment, and balance. Sacrifice balance, and you have no power. Maintain balance, and you have power to spare. This is why Wing Chun is focused on maintaining a balanced body and mind.

Simplicity

"Any intelligent fool can make things bigger, more complex, and more violent. It takes a touch of genius — and a lot of courage to move in the opposite direction." — **Ernst F. Schumacher**

Wing Chun is not flashy. It doesn't look like much, and that's the point. The goal is to do more with less, not do more with more. Any fool can add, but it takes a genius to know when there's nothing left to take away.

Wing Chun is not complicated. When a situation is going down, you don't have time to think about a lot. Your fine motor skills go out the window once adrenaline hits your system. This is why intricate movements that work just fine in class are unworkable in the street.

There are no extraneous movements in Wing Chun. Everything should be as simple and direct as possible. This conserves energy and time, the most precious resources of your life.

Dynamic Tension

If you grew up reading comic books like I did, you probably saw this advertisement somewhere in their pages:

It's perfect. It plays on your fear of not being able to defend yourself; as though muscles alone will keep you safe!

The photograph of the man in the lower left corner is Charles Atlas, who won the title of "The World's Most Perfectly Developed Man." Atlas said the secret to his incredible physique was a regime of physical exercises that used no equipment or weights. He said anyone who followed his advice would get the same results.

He sold a mail-order course explaining exactly what to do and how to do it. Being the curious sort, I bought the course a couple years back and I'm so glad I did. Turns out, the story of how to do the exercises was more important than what exercises you were doing.

Our bodies work because we have two sets of muscles for every joint, basically: one to make it extend out, and one to make it contract in. Charles said if you flexed both sets of muscles so that they were flexing against each other, you'd get stronger.

Imagine you're doing a bicep curl without a dumbell. Instead, you flex your biceps AND your triceps as hard as you can as you move through the motion of the curl. This is what makes it dynamic; you're moving through a full range of motion instead of flexing and holding a pose/ position like you do with an isometric exercise.

When I got his course I realized Charles Atlas was using a method to condition his body (knowingly or not) that martial artists have been using for centuries, just like Wim Hof did for breathing. It's Dynamic Tension.

And it makes sense.

The idea is that as you work out, you get stronger which provides more resistance, which gets you stronger, and so on. Plus, it's incredibly hard to injure yourself because as you get tired, you offer less and less resistance. It's nearly impossible to overload your system.

This is the Chi Gung part of the Wing Chun system. Each form is performed as a Dynamic Tension exercise and as a function of the tension/compression part of Tensegrity. It should feel like there's a black hole at your center of gravity, and your whole body is being compressed more and more as all slack is drawn out of your body.

The real trick is being able to turn on the Dynamic Tension at close range so you can use your whole body to deliver maximum momentum to your opponent but instantly turn it off if they try to pull against you.

Relaxation

If dynamic tension is about strength development, relaxation is about generating power.

It is counterintuitive, but the more relaxed the body can be while performing a posture, the more effective it will be. If it feels strong, that means too much muscular strength has been engaged, and it's like driving a car with the brakes on. Feeling strength is really the perception of your muscles restricting a joint's range of motion.

Cultivating a practice of deep relaxation allows you to apply only the amount of force that is necessary, and no more. It's incredibly efficient that way. Plus, maintaining relaxation constantly reminds you not to meet force with force directly. That would reduce the encounter to a contest of strength. Focusing instead on relaxation will show you the path of least resistance.

Transitions

Every moment is completely unique, and unlike any other moment before it. The eternal now is unchanging and never the same twice. Dynamic Quality can only be experienced *right now*, and it is always available to you.

In fact, you're never out of the moment; otherwise you'd be the world's first time traveler.

Every single posture, detail, or position discussed in this book is a dissection of a living breathing entity; the Dynamic situation. There is no 'perfect posture.' There's only embodied Quality in relationship to the present moment. Since the relationship is ever-changing, so too are the conditions that govern what the ideal postures would be.

When we look at the practical 'how to' section of the book, understand that you're looking at abstracted slivers of time viewed at 1x magnification. As we move more deeply into the changes between two postures, understand it's not the process of flipping a switch, or going from 0 to 1.

It's a gradient. The change could be broken down into infinite points along the way, as Archimedes' second infinity shows us is possible. If you see a posture, a situation, or life as a stark either/or separation, you've already lost. Open your understanding to move beyond the logic of if/then and see the Dynamic situation as infinite possibilities and transitions moving as an interrelated flow.

You'll understand that each transition can flow through multiple vectors simultaneously. The elbow can move up, forward, and rotate all at the same time, and this applies for each joint involved in the posture.

Multiplied together, you can have an incredibly complex compound movement in a seemingly simple posture. When applied to another person, they will find it very difficult to resist as the force feels like it's coming from every angle at the same time but focused on their center of mass.

Breaking *Bridges*

"I don't want to have to sue you" his teacher said. "You're stealing my ideas, and I don't like it."

He was confused. His teacher specifically told him to teach, to share Wing Chun with the world, but here he was being threatened as a thief after years of friendship.

It makes sense, though.

He thought back to several years ago when his teacher briefly told him a story in passing.

His teacher had originally been turned down as a student from a well known and respected instructor. So his teacher convinced his girlfriend to take lessons, and then share what she learned.

In this way he learned by proxy until he revisited the instructor and demonstrated what he knew. The instructor had known what had happened, but admired the dedication and accepted him into the school.

He thought it was only a matter of time until someone who actually did steal teachings accused his own students of doing the same.

The guilty see their crime everywhere they look; especially in those closest to them.

It's a classic narcissist move. Thieves accuse others of stealing from them. Abusers accuse others of abusing them. They will accuse others of taking advantage of them when they prey on their friends and family, themselves.

It was a tough lesson to learn.

His now former teacher wound up blocking him on all avenues of connection, and withdrew his endorsement.
He was excommunicated.

He lost exactly one night of sleep over it. He stayed awake wondering what he should do. Wondering what was going to happen. And then realization dawned.

He can only choose his own path. If he clung to how things had been, it would be nothing but painful.
If, however, he remembered his training he

would recall "No punch, no grab." It's a saying that reminds the Kung Fu student to never allow themselves to compromise their balance by either throwing themselves all into an attack, or holding onto their opponent who can use the connection to pull them off balance.

It could also be said as, "No push, no pull. Just be."

That snapped him out of it.

He let go of his attachment to the need of being validated by his now-former teacher, and decided to focus on his own training. He decided on building a practice that he could be proud of.

After all, that was the only work that mattered.

That's how he learned that sometimes the toughest lesson a teacher can share with a student is that they're not needed any more.

Allow yourself to make and break connections as they serve you. The instant they can harm you, let go. Do not hold onto the pain. Also, the instant a connection tries to pull you off balance, break it.

This is the wisdom of the Chum Kiu form.

Chapter **12**

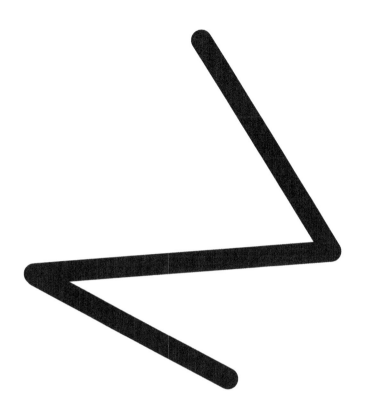

Forms

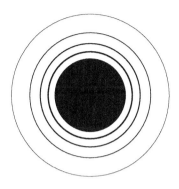

Siu Nim Tau

"Little Idea" or "Little Mind Fist"

It could also be translated as "Focused Mind Power." The form is a mediation on how effective a person can be when their body, mind, breathing, and intention are perfectly aligned on an objective. As the postures are performed, they should be done with a certain mindset. First the intention moves to the destination. Then the feeling of energy moves to the end point, and the body follows. Done in this way the practitioner embodies total personal alignment.

It's a simple idea, but a tough one to embody.

Siu Nim Tau isn't just the first form; it's the

foundation of the entire system. The meaning of 'the little idea' is that you should focus only on that which is important. Simplify to increase your effectiveness. Think of it as the process of defining zero. It is the starting point, and the place that every distance is measure from. In Archimedes' multiple infinities this is the first one.

Zero is the original infinity.

A map is only useful if you know 1) where you're going, but more importantly 2) where you're starting. Siu Nim Tau is the process of defining your placement in the universal map. As you perform the movements in Siu Nim Tau, you are encoding the proprioceptive definition of your own internal zero point.

To use a different metaphor, the Siu Nim Tau form is like building an unassailable castle. People could attack it as much as they want, but the perfect defenses could withstand whatever they send.

But, at the heart of the matter is this: when you're

in the middle of a dynamic situation, the more you have to manage or think about, the more likely you are to lose track of the important details and freak out.

Siu Nim Tau is the simplicity of what's left after every extraneous movement has been burned away from thousands of years of evolutionary pressures, leaving only the ideal ways the human body can align itself to the universal forces of nature.

"Any fool can make something complicated. It takes a genius to make it simple."
— **Woody Guthrie**

The movements and postures aren't fighting techniques themselves, but they are the building blocks that fighting techniques will eventually be built on.

This why Siu Nim Tau is a foundational form; you'll learn it on day one, and still be doing it on your last day on Earth. This is also why it's sometimes called the "Master's Form": even though you learn it first it's the seed that will eventually grow and flourish with the right care and attention given to its progress.

No matter how far the student progresses, their skill will improve by returning to the Siu Nim Tau form. You could study just this form and be a Kung Fu master, as all other forms unfold from its secrets.

Think of the Siu Nim Tau form as the alphabet of the Wing Chun system. To speak any language effectively you have to understand each letter and how to pronounce it. Or, think of it like constructing a high-rise building. You have to build the foundation and the first 99 floors before you can build the 100th floor.

The Siu Nim Tau is the alphabet, foundation, and the simplest structure of Kung Fu. It's the tetrahedron of Wing Chun.

It's also sometimes called "The Little Mind Fist," which I think is fitting. Just as a punch is the dynamic expression of the physical component of "fist," the mind is the dynamic expression of the physical component "brain." To practice the Siu Nim Tau is to encode ideas into your physical form[1].

The more you practice the form, the more ingrained the proper movements and structure will become in your neuromuscular system. This is because every time you perform a complex movement, certain patterns of neurons in your brain fire, which propagate down your spinal cord and travel along your nervous system until the proper muscles are triggered. Eventually, the pathway is reinforced with myelin insulation along its entire length, and that means less of the initial electrical impulse is lost to unimportant pathways. This is what most people call muscle memory, which is a misnomer. Your muscles don't remember, but your neuromuscular pathways do become more efficient at transmitting energy, which we experience and interpret as being "easier."

This neuromuscular process is why the Siu

---

1   And this process transforms the generic human body into the highest Quality tensegrity structure possible.

Nim Tau form is performed very slowly. When you practice slowly, you're only encoding the proper movements. If you go too fast, you'd have too much wobble, noise, fuzz, or inappropriate movements being encoded. Practice slow to learn fast. Practice makes permanent, not perfect, so it's important to have perfect practice. The only way to do that isto go so slowly that you can't mess it up.

Practice the Siu Nim Tau at a glacial pace, and your skills will improve rapidly.

Breakdown

The Siu Nim Tau can be broken down into three main sections.

First: The Opening

This is the transition from everyday posture into Kung Fu posture. It starts from the feet and works its way up your structure to make sure everything is in proper alignment. Your body is engaged, but not tense. Do not gloss over this detail. The beginning posture is the foundation that all other postures depend on. Your arm techniques are only as strong as the base they're built on.

Once your fundamental structure is in place, the form continues by defining the lowest region of space that your arm postures should inhabit, then the highest, and finally the middle.

This divides the space in front of you in half side-to-side along your vertical centerline (left and right), and then into thirds vertically (top, middle, bottom). Now the form introduces the most basic[2] postures like the punch, Tan Sau, Fook Sau, Heun Sau, Pak Sau, Biu Jeet, etc.

Don't worry about what each of those mean now, as we will look at each one in later chapters. For now, we're looking at the way they're practiced in the first segment of the form.

They're done very slowly with full dynamic tension engaged. Core muscles are activated, back muscles are activated, leg muscles: essentially your whole body is engaged

---

2   Which makes them the most essential and important.

through each posture's full range of motion. This establishes muscular strength as well as encouraging strength in connective tissues like tendons and ligaments, which happens at a slower rate than muscle growth.

It's not only for the body; this strengthens your mind, too. When you do this slowly, your mind wants to talk you into going faster. This is your cue to slow down. Focus fully on each excruciatingly slow movement. If the postures are difficult at slow speed, they are impossible to do quickly.

Left, Right

In the first segment, most of the postures are done initially by the left followed by the same sequence on the right. This is as simple as it gets, and beginners still find it challenging. This is the crawling phase of things. There's no extra movement forward and back, side to side, or in rotation. It's simply the postures performed in sequence.

Second Stage

Now that the basics are established, the second

segment ratchets up the difficulty by performing two-handed postures. Both the left and right are doing the same thing at the same time. Also, this is where the form introduces postures that are performed behind the body.

This points to the need to remain mindful of the space surrounding you instead of just what's in front of you. You won't always be facing the problem at the start, so you need to know how to address incoming force even if it is coming at you from a particularly disadvantageous direction — *especially* if it's coming at you at a disadvantageous direction! The system is already showing you how to prepare for the worst case scenario, and giving you the tools to deal with it.

While the first segment defines the boundaries of space in front of you, the second segment defines the boundaries on each side as well as behind you. This is a foreshadowing of what the second form explores more deeply.

Sidenote: *This is another dimension to why the*

Wing Chun system is fractal: The first segment of the Siu Nim Tau is the most basic of the basic.

The second segment of the Siu Nim Tau is slightly more complex, and the ideas here are then explored more deeply (magnified) in the second form: Chum Kiu.

The third segment of the Siu Nim Tau is an introduction to postures that are expressed along more circular pathways than the beginning postures are, which is an idea explored at higher magnification in the third form: Biu Jeet.

The Siu Nim Tau has everything in it, and the rest of the Wing Chun system is designed to explore each of its concepts at deeper levels in later forms.

Chapter **14**

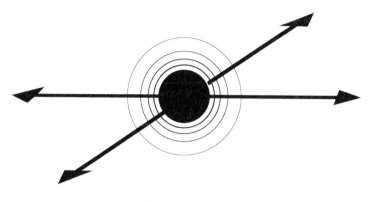

Chum Kiu

"Seeking Bridges" or
"Making and Breaking Bridges"

Your castle can withstand constant attack forever, but the war would be over so much faster if you could ride into battle and attack the opponent directly. This is what Chum Kiu teaches you: how to move to meet the situation.

You are at point A, and your opponent is at point B. What is the best way to close the distance? How do you bridge the gap? Or, when your opponent has made contact that you don't want, how do you break their connection as quickly and thoroughly as possible? This is what Chum Kiu teaches you: how to make and

165

break bridges.

In the Chum Kiu form the student is introduced to the concept of movement along a straight line. The same postures from the Siu Nim Tau form are now performed in concert with footwork that moves forward and back. It's the study of 2-dimensional space; forward / back, and side / side.

Chum Kiu is also where the static Chi Gerk process of leg conditioning in the Siu Nim Tau form turns dynamic. Chum Kiu is the practice of strengthening your legs along with learning the basic footwork required to move your high-Quality Tensegrity structure in 2-dimensional space. Further, you're learning how to use your feet to interrupt, intercept, and apply force, which is a process most people call "kicking."

On a social level Chum Kiu skills are useful for helping you make and maintain high-Quality connections as well as helping you break and prevent low-Quality connections. Without your own high-Quality Tensegrity structure to connect to, or 'personal integrity' for short, all your connections are going to be low-Quality.

Siu Nim Tau is structure, and Chum Kiu is structure moved in straight-line motion.

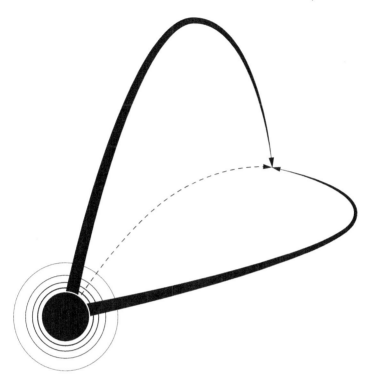

Biu Jeet

"Thrusting Fingers" or "Pointing Finger"

The deadly form! Not to be taught to outsiders! Only shared with the most trusted student, and even then only after they prove their allegiance.

Why all the secrecy? Are the techniques too terrible for mere mortals?

Yes and no.

Wing Chun is a perfect system built on universal principles. If you obey the laws of the universe, you'll never be in trouble. Problem is, you're human. You're not perfect. You cannot maintain perfect alignment with the universe.

You're going to screw up.

And when you're trying to embody the Wing Chun principles, you're going to fail in very specific ways. As Kung Fu evolved, the old masters recognized that the ways to navigate these failures should be baked into the the system, too. It's all well and good to say, "Don't screw up" but we're dealing with a realistic process, after all.

The more reasonable approach is to say, "In a perfect world, you'd never need this stuff, but since you're a Wing Chun practitioner, you're going to screw up in these ways. When you screw up. *When*, not if. Here's what to do about it."

So you can see that part of the longstanding

secrecy of not teaching everyone the Biu Jeet form comes from not wanting to announce your Achilles heel to the world. It would put you at a decided disadvantage from a strategic context, to be sure.

If the Siu Nim Tau is the process of building structure by performing one posture in a slow controlled manner, and Chum Kiu is moving that structure in straight lines while performing a couple techniques on the same plane, then Biu Jeet is the process of moving in curved lines and arcs within a full 3-dimensional context. Biu Jeet footwork is circular. Multiple techniques are executed across several dimensions simultaneously.

The first two forms are practiced with the back straight from start to finish. Biu Jeet has you bend your spine at one point. Where techniques follow the static and dynamic centerline in the first two forms, Biu Jeet techniques crossover centerlines and move in circles while traveling from low-to-high and high-to-low vectors.

The Biu Jeet form seems to violate the bedrock concepts that give birth to the Siu Nim Tau and Chum Kiu forms, but it's actually the natural result of taking those ideas to their logical conclusion.

A straight line is the shortest (and therefore fastest) route between two points, but what happens if the other person is bigger and stronger than you? What happens when you can't plow straight through their defenses? What do you do when the direct approach won't work?

Use the indirect approach. Don't be obvious. Use the circular path. Go around. Be covert. Use deception.

Lie.

Direct overcomes weakness, but indirect overcomes strength. Experience and guile can easily defeat youth and enthusiasm.

Biu Jeet is the form of dirty tricks and last-resort techniques; eye gouges, throat rips, groin strikes, and the like. That is the "thrusting fingers" part of the title. It's the literal interpretation.

The metaphorical interpretation is the pointing finger translation of the title. Biu Jeet, as a form, is pointing to the reality that you're going to wind up in bad situations. You have to look beyond what is currently happening and figure out how you're going to get out of it. It's reminding you to not get lost in the details that will lead to you losing the lesson (and worse, the fight).

This is the intellectual birthplace of my favorite scene from Bruce Lee's movie *"Enter the Dragon."* He is speaking to his student and says, "It's like a finger pointing away to the moon." His student stares intently at his index finger, so Bruce's character slaps the student on the head and says, "Don't concentrate on the finger, or you will miss all that heavenly glory."

Very Zen, but 100% Kung Fu.

Why wait so long to introduce these ideas? Why not address the worst-case scenarios right away? It's easier to teach the exceptions to the rules if the student already understands the rules completely. The Biu Jeet form is only useful after the student has fully integrated the concepts and movements from the first two forms.

"Learn the rules like a pro, so you can break them like an artist." —**Pablo Picasso**

Chapter **16**

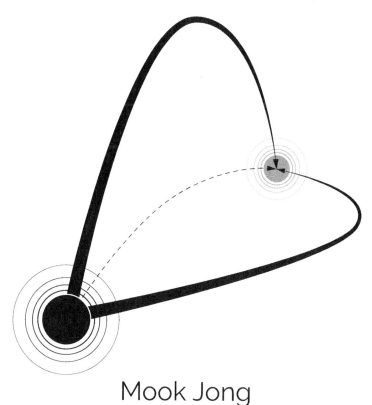

Mook Jong

"Wooden Dummy"

The Mook Jong is the first apparatus form of the Wing Chun system. It's basically an upright log with three wooden "arms" and a single "leg" sticking out of it. Sometimes it's mounted on the wall, but it can also be a freestanding setup, too. Basically, it's the Wing Chun student's training partner, which is why it's called the Wooden Dummy.

177

Don't be fooled, however. He's a lot smarter than you.

The arms and leg are positioned at precise angles that are better than any human defender could ever have. Each arm could represent an opponent's left arm, right arm, outside arm, inside arm, etc. It's many hyper-states represented in elegant simplicity. The idea is to use the Mook Jong as a precision instrument to apply techniques so you can learn distance management, positioning, and how to transition from technique to technique.

When you apply a technique and it hits the Mook Jong, you know that the dummy is going to win every time. There's no sense in trying to push through the arm. Instead, you learn to respond to your postures meeting resistance by transitioning to a different position in relationship to the dummy. This naturally leads to a different posture as your relationship to the dummy changes, too.

This is Chi Sau. It is also Chin Na[1].

1   The Mook Jong form is a grappling form performed while standing. It shows you how to prevent takedowns, how to trip your opponent, move to the blind side, and how to free yourself if trapped on the ground, too. Too few Wing Chun instructors recognize its

Page 178

You learn how close or far away you should be standing from the dummy to perfectly deliver a technique. If you're standing too close, it won't work. If you're standing too far away, it won't work. If you're too far to the right, it won't work. If you're too far to the left, it won't work.

You quickly get a feel for what distance is just beyond kicking range, where optimal kicking range is, where punching range starts, the best distance where elbow strikes do maximum damage, where trapping range transitions into grappling, and so on.

It's an incredibly versatile tool that functions as your exercise, training, and sparring partner all rolled into one.

Put the Mook Jong in your living room, and you have a training partner who is ready to play 24/7 and never gets tired. This is how the Wing Chun practitioner can turbo-charge their skillset without having to worry about comparing calendars with a partner, traveling to a gym, or worrying about a partner's ego grappling wisdom.

getting the better of them and landing a sucker punch "just for fun."

I can't tell you how many people I've talked with over the years who tell me they "used to do Brazilian Jiu Jitsu" until someone popped their knee or elbow joint during a rolling session. With a Mook Jong, that can never happen. The Wooden Dummy might be tough, but it can only hurt you if you attack it[2] and it is perfectly devoid of ego.

Siu Nim Tau establishes your high-Quality Tensegrity structure. Chum Kiu teaches you how to move it. Biu Jeet shows you how to navigate through and beyond worst-case conditions. Mook Jong introduces you to managing Dynamic Relationships across spacetime.

Welcome to the 4th dimension.

---

2   A very powerful Kung Fu lesson, indeed.

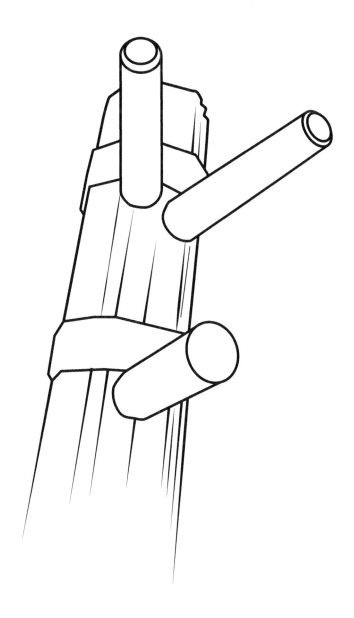

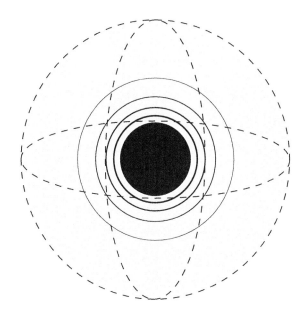

Bart Jam Dao

"8 Slash Knives"

You've created a high-Quality Tensegrity structure. You know how to move it while maintaining balance and control. You know how to move in and through bad situations. You know how to manage the relationship between you and an opponent, and you can recognize outside distance, kicking, punching, elbow and knee, trapping, and grappling ranges.

Now you're ready to add weapons.

The title points to the eight vectors that the knives travel in the Bart Jam Dao form, but there aren't many new concepts to learn. Like the four previous forms, the fifth is an unfolding of the concepts first introduced in the Siu Nim Tau. The only difference between this one and the first is you're holding two large war knives instead of empty fists. The basic ideas stay the same.

The short swords effectively extend your range of influence. For the first time, you can reach beyond the limits of your own hands and feet. You're finally human; you're using tools. Many of the two-handed movements are taken directly from the Biu Jeet form, but they're slightly modified to accommodate the foot-long swords. The structure stays the same, but their interrelationships shift ever so slightly.

Now, are you likely to be carrying war knives in a day to day setting? Probably not. So why should you learn this form? If for no other reason, it's great exercise for your wrists. Swinging swords around in a controlled fashion is a hell of a workout. It helps cultivate strong tendons and ligaments at a notoriously weak link in the biomechanical chain.

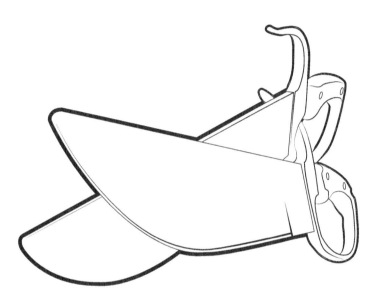

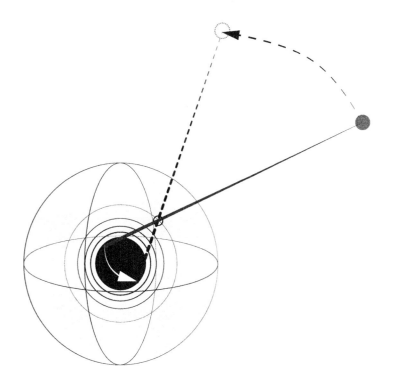

Luk Dim Boon Kwan

"6½ point pole"

You have a structure. You can move it in straight lines. You also know how to move in curves, and you can move it through 4-dimensional space. You also have begun increasing your area of influence with tools.

Now you're ready to wield a 9-foot long pole

made out of hardwood.

That means it's heavy as hell, and your forearms are going to be ripped.

And, that's the secret: it's a powerful workout.

You aren't usually going to be walking through your daily life with a 9-foot pole, but the strength you develop while training with it will serve you well.

The form has no twirling, no spinning, and none of the fun moves you tried when you were 12 using a broom handle. Since the pole is so long, you handle it more like a spear. Tight curves and straight thrust attack is the name of the game.

But, the hidden lesson is the power of leverage.

With the sword form, you learn how to increase your direct influence, but the pole form teaches you how to use leverage to create massive effects across space and time with very little movement on your part.

The problem is, it takes massive strength to apply it accurately and not allow the lever to pull you off balance. Fortunately, that's exactly what this form does: it gets you strong! Such is the power of leverage.

"Give me the place to stand, and I shall move the earth."
~Archimedes, Kung Fu Master talking about leverage.

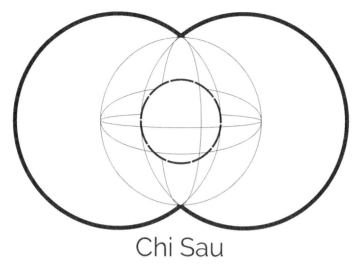

Chi Sau

"Sticky Hands"

Chi Sau is not a form, per se, but it is one of the most important exercises in the system, so I'm including it here. As I mentioned in the 4 Elements of Kung Fu section, the purpose of Chi Sau drills is to cultivate a physical sensitivity to the intentions and actions of your opponent by making direct contact.

In order to maximize the skill, you need a laboratory where sensitivity is the only changing variable. To start, you have two participants who have their own prescribed sequence of three postures in a relatively static dynamic. It's a collaborative choreography so both people don't have to spend mental energy on trying to figure out what's next; they know their part, and they know their partner's part. Also, they're both out of striking range. This is to eliminate the worry of "are they going to hit me?!" No, they're not.

All you have to worry about is feeling how much pressure the other person is applying to your structure with theirs, and how to feel when they're changing that pressure by initiating their next movement.

Think about an amoeba. It has a cell membrane, or a boundary, if you will. If you introduce a negative stimulus, like sulphuric acid, its boundary can immediately discern the low-Quality environment and the amoeba will move away from it. The longer the amoeba takes to perceive the low-Quality dynamic, the less time it has to respond before being affected by the situation.

Touch sensitivity is an ancient sense, while vision is relatively recent. Vision is also very processor-heavy, which means it takes several hundred milliseconds longer for your brain to make sense of what it's seeing than it does to understand what it's feeling.

This is why looking at your dance partner's feet never works. By the time you see what they're doing, it's too late. You have to feel what they're doing and respond to that. If you have proper frame, as they say in the ballroom dancing world, as soon as you make contact with your dance partner you know exactly where all their parts are, how they're moving, and which direction they're moving in.

Touch is massively more useful in this context than vision, and that's why you can dance with your eyes closed even though there's another person involved.

Same goes for a dynamic confrontation. The more sensitive your sense of touch is, the quicker you can respond to the intention of your opponent. You practice it by rote in the first stage of Chi Sau, and then more dynamically in the second level where both arms are involved but movements aren't pre-set. Finally, you have something that is more akin to sparring than a drill, but that's only useful after you've spent the time working on the foundational Chi Sau skill.

If you consistently work on your Chi Sau skill by working with the beginning Chi Sau exercise, you'll learn how to outmaneuver anyone who mainly relies on vision to keep track of their opponent and ignores the wealth of information that a single touch will give you. You'll also be more comfortable with close-quarters contact, and be able to maximize your Chin Na skills of trapping at this range, too.

Then, once you're familiar with what skill the exercise is designed to cultivate, a little more chaos can be added to the system. The second-level Chi Sau drill is more free flowing, and the name of the game is to get the other partner to move by either pushing or pulling them, or allowing them to push or pull themselves off balance. If either student has to step in order to move their partner, they lose. After all, in a fight, everyone should be able to do two things: 1) Stand their ground. 2) Keep their hands up.

To begin, both partners stand facing each other within striking distance[1]. Both arms are extended and make connection. Either student can do whatever they want as long as they stay connected[2]. Then it's game on. Push, pull, resist, yield, whatever the student needs to do to thwart the training partner's force.

The more time spent practicing second level Chi Sau, the more sensitive the Wing Chun structure becomes. It's like when I first started to learn how to partner dance. I was completely unaware of my partner's momentum and force as it influenced my balance, but eventually I got to the point where I only needed a light touch to lead my partner.

This is what Chi Sau develops: a hair trigger to

---

1   This is closer together than the first level Chi Sau drill where the student doesn't have to worry about contact being made. Now, there's contact.

2   Some schools allow touching the face, but I prefer only chest shots. They're harder to land than face hits, and if you do get a solid tag to the chest you and your partner both know their face would have been even easier.

maintain boundaries. It allows the Wing Chun practitioner to be aware of outside force more quickly, perceive its line of intent, and know what direction to send it in order to maintain the boundary. It does this by putting the student in a more dynamic situation while not allowing absolute chaos. As ability and confidence improve, the training allows more chaos by introducing footwork, or beginning with partners not touching to become familiar with establishing contact.

What Chi Sau isn't is "chasing hands." Some Wing Chun students become so enamored with deflecting their partner's hands that they forget to probe and question their partner's boundaries. The goal in a dynamic situation isn't to play patty-cake with an attacker; it is to make contact as quickly and effectively as possible. It is when a technique meets an obstruction that the Chi Sau skill really shines. If the initial path is not viable, what would be the best option? Chi Sau can identify the best alternative.

So if the Wing Chun fighter doesn't want to just

stick to the opponent's limbs, why is it called "sticky hands?" Because the opponent feels like the Wing Chun fighter's structure is constantly applying pressure to their center mass where the Wing Chun fighter's force can do the most damage. The other fighter will feel like the Wing Chun man is water looking for a crack in the sidewalk to flow into. Chi Sau is less about defense, and more about attack and applying constant pressure.

Or, as the most famous teacher of Wing Chun, Yip Man would say, "Greet what arrives, escort what leaves, and rush upon loss of contact." Don't fight force head-on and don't get caught up following the opponent's movements. If they make the mistake of disengaging and freeing up your hand, let it fly to their face!

Multi-Dimensional Chi Sau

This is a practical exercise that focuses on the physical dynamic, but it also has application beyond the body's limits. These concepts of boundary awareness and perceiving force against it also applies to intellectual, emotional, interpersonal, and professional dimensions, too

Overview

That's the whole system in a nutshell. Each form has its own purpose and intention behind its creation. Moving to the next form is useless until the practitioner has a firm grasp of the fundamental concept embedded in the present form. Building a second floor is impossible until the first level is built.

Focus on the first thing and build a structure (Siu Nim Tau), learn how to move it along straight lines (Chum Kiu), then move it in curved pathways (Biu Jeet), and apply the structure in four dimensions (Mook Jong) before using tools to increase effectiveness (Bart Jam Dao), and apply leverage (Luk Dim Boon Kwan), before finally developing the sensitivity to know what is happening, know what to do about it, and when to do it (Chi Sau).

With focused effort and dedication a person can acquire the whole system in about nine months, but spend the rest of their life unfolding the treasure they were handed.

Plus, there are tons of variations to the forms you can use when you get bored, but you'll always find yourself coming back to the basics.

Such is practice, and such is life.

PRACTICE

prac·tice

praktəs/*noun*

1: the actual application or use of an idea, belief, or method as opposed to theories about such application or use.

The Good Stuff

Alright! Enough theory. Enough ideas. Now we get to the actual postures, themselves. Or, as I think about it, the embodiments of these universal concepts of geometry and Quality we've been talking about this whole time.

What follows is a glossary of sorts. These are the basic postures that comprise the physical alphabet of martial arts and self-defense. These are the pieces that flow together in infinite combinations in accordance with the principles of centerline, balance, Yin & Yang, etc. to make what we call techniques.

Look at any black-belt level Jiu Jitsu technique on YouTube and you will find these postures again and again. Also, it's important to note; there are no perfect postures. They are no magic bullets. Each posture is most useful in a particular relationship with a particular direction of force, and as such they are a sliver of time instead of a distinct technique.

Gee Kim Yeung Ma

"Figure two goat catching stance"

TRADITIONAL

Imagine a goat tried running between your legs and you want to squeeze your knees together to trap the goat. This is the basic idea behind why you're standing this way. Why is "figure two" in the name, too? If you drew a line connecting your feet, and a line connecting your knees while in the stance, you'd get the Chinese character for "2."

The basic stance is not meant for fighting. It's a training stance that develops the legs as well as putting your body in a zero impact relationship that gets you stronger through isometric and dynamic tension applications. Head over shoulders, shoulders over hips, hips over feet.

Feet are barely past shoulder width and the toes are pointed in at a point 3 feet in front of your centerline. Knees are brought in slightly, and abs and hip flexors are activated to tuck your butt under your spine[1]. Think of the feet pointing inward as the start of focusing your intention to the point in front of you.

---

1   If your pelvis was a cup full of wine, you're going to tilt the cup so wine would pour out the back. A posterior pelvic tilt.

Fists are turned with the palms to the ceiling, and are positioned by the nipples without touching the sides of the body. Shoulder blades are pulled back to point the elbows straight behind you. Shoulders are lowered and locked in place.

This is the basic training stance. Some people find it uncomfortable at first, and here's why: the stance shows you where your body is already hurt. It, itself, does not aggravate your body. The stance is a simple baseline that will highlight any areas of your body that are severely out of alignment as the result of poor posture, sitting habits, or other reasons.

As such, problems that have gone unrecognized can quickly become apparent as you try to maintain the basic stance. If you blame the stance, you're missing the point completely. Use it as a diagnostic tool to understand where you're going wrong in your day-to-day life and then you'll know what to change.

This detail alone is worth the price of the book.

Man Sau
"Asking Hand"

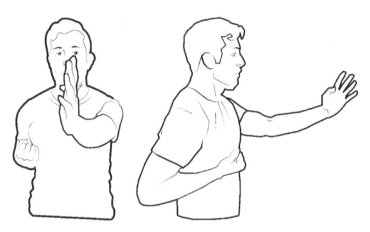

Think of Donnie Yen playing Yip Man, standing in the ready-to-fight stance. One hand held out, one hand midway between the outer hand and his chest. The outer hand is Man Sau.

If it's the Asking Hand, it makes sense to wonder, "What is it asking?"

Good question.

Mainly it's used to ask the opponent, "What are

you going to let me do? Are you going to let me touch your center?" It's a constant "shit test" for your opponent.

Man Sau is the first line of physical contact. It's the earliest opportunity you have to redirect your opponent's intention. How your opponent answers your Man Sau tells you everything you need to know.

And as my Mom told me growing up, "If you never ask, you'll never know."

Wu Sau

"Protecting Hand"

This is the hand held halfway between your Man Sau and your body. It's there just in case your opponent gets past your first line of inquiry. If he does, you have a backup hand to deal with it.

From the traditional ready stance of the Man Sau and Wu Sau position, the rest of the postures naturally flow from the encounter. Here are the main ones you'll find yourself using the most.

Tan Sau

"Dividing Hand"

If someone was trying to punch you, but you kept ducking behind a street sign, they'd have to go around the pole to get to you. This is the basic idea of this posture. Present Tan Sau along the dynamic centerline, and it forces the opponent to go around because two objects cannot occupy the same space at the same time. The forearm is extended at a 45-degree angle with the elbow pointed at the floor and positioned towards the static centerline and a fist width's distance away from the body.

Tan Sau is very strong in relationship with forces coming straight at it. The forearm works like a train's cow catcher; the 45-degree angle forcing incoming energy to glance off into a safe direction[2].

Bong Sau

"Wing Arm"

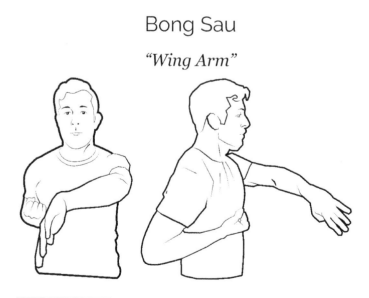

---

2   Away from your face.

Looking much like the wing of bird, Bong Sau gets its name from the momentary transition from a posture like Tan Sau to redirect incoming force like a punch away from its path before the elbow is quickly brought back down to its usual position where it can protect your body's static centerline.

To execute a basic Bong Sau, think about looking at a wristwatch. The thumb turns towards the floor, the palm faces away from you, the elbow rises away from your ribs, and your forearm bends at the elbow at a 45 degree angle. Now bend your palm forward at the wrist so that your fingers point directly towards your opponent, and you have it.

Your structure remains compressed and sensitive while your hand stays relaxed. This static version of the posture is the most basic version of it as it is introduced in the Siu Nim Tau form. Horizontal movement is added to the Bong Sau in the Chum Kiu form and curves are added in Biu Jeet, but all the variations are only as strong as the one you build in the static version.

Fook Sau

"Covering Hand"

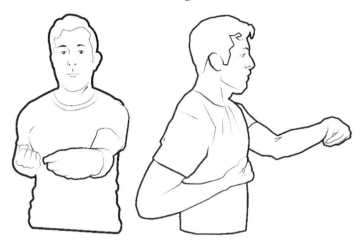

This peculiar posture looks ridiculous, but is actually quite genius. The wrist bends in with the fingers together like a beak while the elbow bends in towards the static centerline.

The crook of the wrist functions as a way to control someone's arm without having to hold on. This way, if the opponent quickly pulls their hand down, you are not pulled off balance. Their lack of connection frees your hand to instantly seek its target: their face. They made the mistake of disengaging without protecting their angles, and who are you to protect them from the law of cause and effect? Just remember, when the

213

Fook Sau loses connection, let your posture spring forward like an arrow released and change your hand into a fist on the way to the target.

When force is applied from the bottom going upward, however, the Fook Sau posture is very strong. Think of it like paper covering rock but it's Fook Sau covering uppercut (Tan Sau with a fist).

It is also useful in arm bars, cross arm drags, and a whole host of grappling applications. Much more versatile than you might think at first.

Straight Punch

"The 'From Here to Face' Hand"

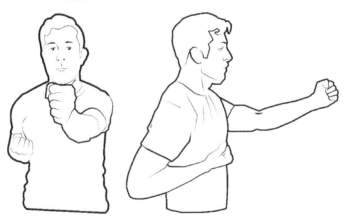

Instantly recognizable by the vertical orientation of the fist: thumb toward the ceiling and elbow pointed at the ground. When delivered, the fist travels along the static centerline (which should be in alignment with the dynamic centerline) like an arrow flying to the opponent's center of mass.

It is treated like a battering ram delivered with the full weight of the body behind it. In order to increase its effect, the whole body is moved forward, which adds momentum to the posture.

If the punch is intercepted or pushed offline, it naturally transforms into any one of the other Wing Chun postures. This is why the punching arm is sensitive. Relaxation is the name of the game.

Most people tense the muscles in their arm when punching because it makes the punch feel stronger. What they're actually doing is trying to make up for poor structural alignment with muscles. The result is like driving a car with the brakes on; it will never reach top speed.

This is why the most powerful punches are done quickly and with the minimum amount of muscular tension required to keep them on track.

Heun Sau

"Circling Hand"

As we covered in Biu Jeet, "Direct overcomes weakness, but indirect overcomes strength," and that's exactly what Heun Sau is all about. It gets you around immovable obstacles through its circular movement.

Heun Sau is done with the wrist and when done properly it strengthens the tendons and connective tissue in your arm. In a fighting context, however, the circular motion performed with the hand works like the head of a snake allowing your arm to wind around the opponent's limb without having to retract and re-engage[3].

---

3   Thereby losing precious time traveling all that distance.

This is useful for getting from the inside to the outside, or vice versa. It is also incredibly effective at bleeding off force coming directly at you. If your opponent is punching straight at you, and you can Heun Sau with it, then the punch will easily be deflected into a broad circular arc instead of a straight line.

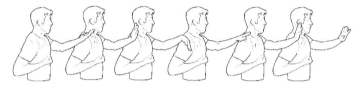

Pak Sau

"Slapping Hand"

Often thought of as a deflection tool, I like to think of Pak Sau more as a "clapping hand," which describes the right feel. Thinking of it like a slapping hand seems to imply a quick slap and retract action. Clapping has a more solid essence to it. Contact is made firmly, deeply, and penetrates to the floor. It's less slap and more open-handed strike applied to an opponent's punch.

It's applied at a 45-degree angle away from the body, and a 45-degree angle up from the ground. This ensures as much coverage as possible, and improves the chances of catching the opponent's attack. Pak Sau never moves beyond the shoulder. To do so would leave you open to having your arm pinned against your body as it crosses the static centerline. Pak Sau only moves as much as it has to to deflect, and no more than that.

Its aim is more toward the opponent's elbow. If you make contact too near the opponent's wrist, he could easily Heun Sau around the Pak Sau, and you lose. If you control his elbow, however, mobility of his arm is severely limited.

A useful combination is to redirect your opponent's arm with a solid Pak Sau, and thread a Tan Sau along the outer part of your Pak Sau's forearm to continue the redirection. This leaves the Pak Sau free to attack directly as a straight punch.

Biu Sau

"Darting Hand"

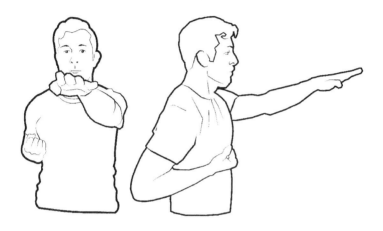

Thrusting fingers, darting hand, whatever. It doesn't matter what it's called when it pokes your eyes out.

Can also be applied to the throat or other soft targets, but is usually reserved for dire circumstances.

Jut Sau

"Sinking Hand"

Woe unto the tense fighter. Too many people allow their whole body to tense up before and during a fight. Their arms are held rigid, which they think means is a stronger barrier. To us, however, it means it's super easy to pull them off balance as they've conveniently made their whole body a single unit, like a piece of wood balanced on end.

When you make contact and feel they're too stiff, you'll use a Jut Sau. It's a sharp little quick downward impulse that can be surprisingly effective at completely disrupting their balance.

The pulse is led by the elbow, which is held lower than the wrist. The movement begins by your elbow and the power is felt in the opponent through the point of contact at your wrist.

Can be used to pull the opponent into a quick eye gouge, a throat grab, or any number of options you have to choose from when it's effective.

Chapter 23

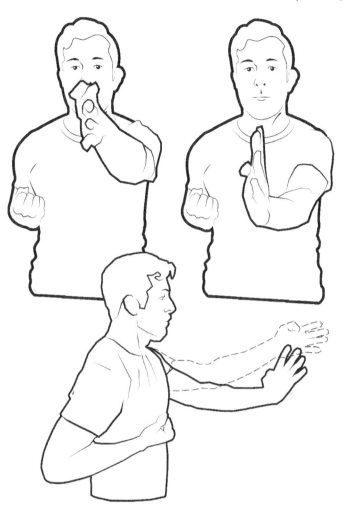

Lap Sau

"Pulling Hand"

If Jut Sau is a downward impulse, then Lap Sau is a horizontal one. Lap Sau is often used not against a resisting opponent, but one who is already moving towards you. Lap Sau adds a little more sauce than they were expecting, and gets them too far ahead of themselves.

Just like the Jut Sau, too, the Lap Sau can be applied and directly transitioned into a punch, or open handed strike against the face or throat.

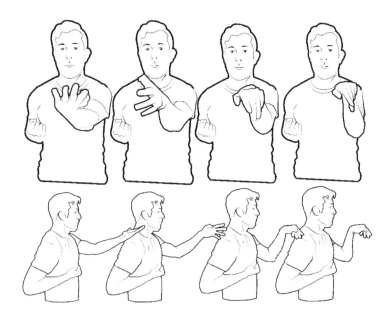

Took Sau

"Lifting Hand"

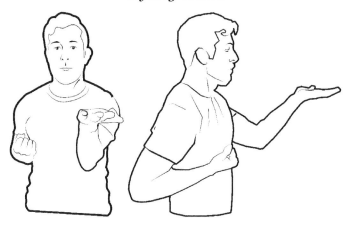

If you're short, you'll find this one especially handy. It's a useful technique for popping an opponent's limb upward which frees you up to rush in underneath for a takedown, floating rib strike, or whatever you like.

Also if the opponent foolishly grabbed you and you step back quickly to straighten their arm, a simple pop to their elbow from underneath would wreak havoc. That's Took Sau.

Lan Sau

"Barring Hand"

The forearm is held horizontally in front of you with a 90° bend in the elbow.

Both arms held this way provide an incredibly strong barrier which is useful if someone is trying to bear hug you or otherwise collapse your space. Slam someone through a wall with double Lan Sau.

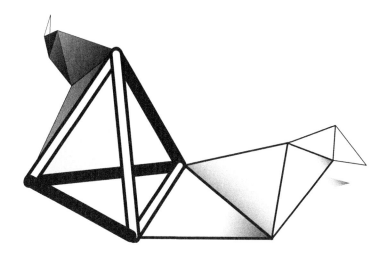

Conclusion

As you've probably figured out by now, all those stories between chapters are autobiographical.

I wanted to show you how many ways I've screwed up, and the many ways the lessons I've learned from my practice of Wing Chun have helped me create boundaries, maintain them, and level up my integrity in a way that I know in the depth of my being.

You can do the same.

Hopefully by now, you've seen how powerful the Wing Chun system is for dealing with every dimension of what it means to be human. It's the crucible that forges all other virtue. It's the bedrock the rest of your life can be built on.

There's nothing else like it.

If you're interested in starting, or gaining depth to your existing practice, I'd love to work with you. Visit the website and connect with me there.

I look forward to hearing from you.

WingChun.Life

ABOUT THE **AUTHOR**

Jonathan Pritchard is a corporate skills trainer, executive coach, keynote speaker on the psychology of elite performance, and world-touring Mentalist for 20+ years who has entertained the troops stationed overseas, performed in Las Vegas, appeared on national TV, and consulted for the best in the business.

He is also a life-long martial arts enthusiast & autodidact. Additionally, he is the author of several books on mindset and motivation including "[think] **Like A Mind Reader**," "Perfect **Recall**," and "[Learn] **Like A Mind Reader**."

When not on the road you can find him training by the lake in Chicago.

INVITATION

If you've made it this far, and are interested in starting your own path to living a Wing Chun life, I invite you to get in touch with me.

I will walk you through my trademark "**E⁴ Training System**" and how we can blend 21st century technology with the most incredible life integration technology known to man: Wing Chun.

thrive@wingchun.life

Printed in Great Britain
by Amazon